12-C

SECURITY ANALYSIS AND PORTFOLIO MANAGEMENT

SECURITY ANALYSIS
AND
PORTFOLIO MANAGEMENT

By

Prof. V. Gangadhar

ANMOL PUBLICATIONS PVT. LTD.

NEW DELHI - 110 002 (INDIA)

ANMOL PUBLICATIONS PVT. LTD.
H.O.: 4374/4B, Ansari Road, Darya Ganj,
New Delhi-110 002 (India)
Ph.: 23278000, 23261597
B.O.: No. 1015, Ist Main Road, BSK IIIrd Stage
IIIrd Phase, IIIrd Block
Bangalore - 560 085 (India)
Visit us at: www.anmolpublications.com

Security Analysis and Portfolio Management

First Edition, 2003

Reprint, 2007

PRINTED IN INDIA

Printed at Mehra Offset Press, Delhi.

ACKNOWLEDGEMENTS

My special thanks are due to our friends and colleagues in the Department of Commerce & Business Management who have been constantly encouraging and motivating to write this text book, which is very useful for the students of BBM, MBA, MFA, MFC, CA, ICWA, Courses of various profession programmes in Management, Open University and Distance Mode.

I sincerely thank my research scholar Dr. M. Yadagiri, Lecturer in Commerce, Lal Bahadur College, Warangal, for his excellent support for preparation of this book. I also thank Dr. G. Ramesh, Lecturer in Commerce, SSR & J College, Khammam, for his help and assistance.

I thank my friends and colleagues Prof. V. Gopal Reddy, Principal, University Arts & Science College, Prof. G. Damodar, Director, Students Welfare Centre, Kakatiya University, Dr. P. Amaraveni, Mr. S.N. Chary, Mr. G. Naresh and Mr. K. Rajender for their constant support and timely help. I also thank M/s. Surya Graphics, Hanamkonda, for the efficient secretarial help.

It is my prime responsibility to thank my wife, Mrs. V. Arunavathi, daughters, Pranathi, Pavani and son Pramod, for having put with the inconveniences caused while writing this book.

I am indebted to Mr. J.L. Kumar for Anmol Publications Pvt. Ltd., New Delhi, for taking the responsibility of publishing the book within a short time.

—**Dr. V. Gangadhar**

PREFACE

The security analysis and portfolio management is one of the key areas of Investment Management, which guides the investors to understand, analyse and make a decision for selecting best set of portfolio. Further, it also enables the financial analysis portfolio managers to make a decision about the investment pattern and its related risk and return.

The investment in portfolio is based on various considerations as well as the risk and reward assumed by the investors. A proper knowledge and skills in the area of Security Analysis and Portfolio Management will be a great help to the investors to make proper decisions. This book will help to overcome the problems faced by various people in this direction.

This book is written in a student-friendly manner, so that the students can read and assimilate the subject matter presented in a lucid manner. This book will greatly be useful to the students of M.Com., MBA, MFA, ICFA, HRM, MFC, CA, ICWA and the students of various Schools of Distance Learning and Open Universities. It will also be beneficial to the financial executives who want to update their knowledge in Security Analysis and Portfolio Management.

This book is divided into 12 chapters, first four are devoted to Securities Analysis such as Concept, Fundamentals, Technical Analysis and Efficient Market Hypothesis. The next four chapters cover the portfolio Analysis and Management,

Portfolio Selection, Portfolio Investment Process and Measurement of Portfolio Performance. The remaining four chapters are aimed at covering mutual funds, financial derivatives, futures and options and swaps.

In order to cater to the needs of Post-Graduate students, Research Scholars and Financial Executives the subject matter is dealt with conceptual and analytical approach. At the end of each chapter a summary along with model short and essay questions is presented. Hence, it will help the reader to develop skills to understand, analyse and point out analytical techniques of securities for an effective selection of portfolio.

—Dr. V. Gangadhar
Professor of Commerce &
Business Management and
Controller of Examinations
Kakatiya University
Warangal (A.P.) 506 009

CONTENTS

1
SECURITY ANALYSIS

OBJECTIVES

The objectives of this lesson are to:

- explain the meaning, objectives and need for security analysis
- highlight the various approaches to security analysis.

1.1 Introduction

The term investment is a word of many meanings. The investment refers to net additions to the capital stock of the community. Investment decision is a part of our economic life. Everybody takes such decisions in different context and at different times. The investor deploys money in specific investment channels with the objective of better returns. The investor has various alternative investment avenues. Savings are invested in assets depending on their risk and return characteristic. All investments are risky. An intelligent investor with skills of management of investment can reduce the risk and maximise returns.

1.2. Concepts of Security Analysis

Security analysis refers to the analysis of trading securities.

It analyses the share price returns and the risk involved in the investment. Every investment involves the risk and the expected return is related to the risk. The security analysis will help in understanding the behaviour of security prices and the market.

Security analysis refers to the analysis of securities from the point of view of their prices, returns and risks. The analysis of risk and return related to the securities will help in understanding the behaviour of security prices, market and decision making for investment. If the analysis includes scrip it is called microanalysis of a company. If it is an analysis of a market with various securities it is known as macro picture of the behaviour of the market. The entire process of estimating return and risk of a security is known as security analysis.

The traditional investment analysis when applied to securities emphasizes the projection of prices and dividends are known as security analysis. It involves the potential price of a share and future dividend stream is forecast, then discounted back to the present value. Such value is called as "Intrinsic Value". Then the intrinsic value is compared with the securities market price. If the current market price is lower than the intrinsic value, then purchase is recommended. Alternatively, if the current market price is higher than the intrinsic value, a sale is recommended. Further, the security analysis is built around the idea that investors are concerned with two principal properties inherent in securities, the return that can be expected from holding a security, and risk that the return is achieved will be less than the return that was expected.

Generally, the investors are interested primarily in selling a security for more than they pay for it. The investor hopes to achieve a higher reward than simply placing the money in a savings account. An investor who seeks reward that exceeds those available on savings account forces the real risk. There is no return without risk. The process of estimating return and risk for individual securities is known as "Security Analysis". Security analysis is the essence of the valuation of financial instruments. The value of financial asset depends upon their return and risk. The universal fact is that everyone must recognise the risk component in investment decision.

1.3 Objectives of Security Analysis

The following are the objectives of Security Analysis:

(i) To estimate the risk and return related to a security.

(ii) To find out the intrinsic value of the security with a view to make a buy/sell decision.

(iii) To identify the under valued securities to buy or over value securities to sell.

(iv) To analyse the stock market trends to understand the market pattern and behaviour.

(v) To forecast the future earnings and dividends along with the price of the securities.

(vi) To find out the key determinants of intrinsic value.

(vii) To analyse and point out the position of economy industry and the company with a view to select the best possible company for investment.

1.4 Need for Securities Analysis

The primary motive for buying a stock is to sell it subsequently at a higher price. The dividends and price changes are the principal ingredients for the expected return of an investor. If the investors are able to know well in advance the information and the about dividends and stock prices over subsequent periods he will gain by selling his securities. However, the world of investing is influenced by political, economical, social and other forces that the investor cannot predict and understand. Therefore, the security analysis helps the investor to determine dividends to be paid on a stock in the future and what the stock price will be in the future.

King observed that on the average over half the variations

in the stock prices could be attributable to a market influence that affects all stock market indices. Therefore, the security analysis has become an essential for the investors to understand and determine the future price prospect of the securities in view of the following:

(i) To estimate stock price changes by probing the forces operating in the overall economy, as well as influences to peculiar to industries.

(ii) To predict the national economy, because economic activity affects the corporate profit, investor attitudes and expectation and ultimately security prices.

(iii) To establish linkages between economic activity and stock market, because the overall economic activity manifests itself in the behaviour of stocks in general.

(iv) To select the right time and right securities for the investment.

The above aspects are important for the security analysts or investors to know the price of stocks and their related risk. Further, the security analysis is needed to understand the following for selecting the right type of securities at right time at right market.

(i) Understanding the macro economic environment and developments.

(ii) Analysis the prospect of the industry to which the firm belongs.

(iii) Assessing the projected performance of the company.

1.5 Approaches to Securities Analysis

The Security analysis aimed at identifying under valued securities to buy and over valued securities to sell. It involves the entire process of estimating return and risk for an individual security.

It is deeply rooted in fundamental concepts to measure the risk and return of a security. It emphasizes on the return and risk estimates rather than mere price and dividend estimates. However, the return and risk estimates are depended on share prices and accompanying dividend stream.

Any forecast of security must necessarily consider the prospects of the economy. The economic sets greatly influence the prospects of certain industries as well as the psychological aspect of the investing public.

The approaches for securities analysis are broadly grouped into the following categories.

(i) Fundamental Analysis

(ii) Technical Analysis

(iii) Efficient Market Hypothesis.

(i) Fundamental Analysis

The first major analysis of securities analysis is the fundamental analysis. A fundamental analysis is a time honoured value based approach depending upon a careful assessment of the fundamental of an economy, industry and the company. The fundamental analysis studies the general economic situation makes an evaluation of an industry and finally does an in-depth analysis of both financial and non-financials of the company of choice. The fundamental analysis is aimed at analysing the various fundamentals or basic factors that affect the risk return of the securities. The fundamental analysis involves the analysis of the following:

(a) The Economic Analysis

(b) The Industry Analysis

(c) The Company Analysis

The Economic Analysis

In the Economic Analysis the investor has to analyse the economic factors to forecast of the economy in order to identify the likely growth of the economy and its trend. Further, based on the economic analysis the investor will identify the industry groups which are promising in the coming years in order to choose the best company in such industry group. The economic analysis provides the investor to develop a sound economic understanding and be able to interpret the impact of important economic indicators on stock markets.

Industry Analysis

The objective of the Industry Analysis is to assess the prospects of various industrial groupings. The industry analysis helps to identify the industries with a potential for future growth and to select companies from such industry to invest in its securities. The industry analysis involves industry life cycle analysis, investment implication, structure and characteristics of an industry.

The Company Analysis

Company Analysis is the last leg in the economy, industry and company analysis sequence. The company analysis is a study of variables that influence the future of a firm both qualitatively and quantitatively. The purpose of the company analysis is to know the intrinsic value of a share of a company.

(ii) The Technical Analysis

As an approach to investment analysis, technical analysis is radically different from fundamental analysis. The technical analysis is frequently used as a supplement to fundamental analysis is, concerned with a critical study of the daily or weekly price volume data of index comprising several shares. The technical analysis analyses the buying and selling pressure, which govern the price trend. It helps the investors to buy cheap and sell high, regardless of the type of company the investor chooses. The technical analysis complies a study of the market itself and not of the various external factors which affect the market. According to technical analyst, all relevant factors get reflected in the volume of the stock exchange transaction and the level of share prices.

The Differences between Technical Analysis and Fundamental Analysis

The differences between Technical Analysis and Fundamental Analysis are presented below:

i) Technical analysis mainly predicts short-term price movements, whereas fundamental analysis tries to establish long term value.

ii) The focus of technical analysis mainly on internal market data, particularly price and volume data. The focus of the fundamental analysis is on fundamental factors relating to the economy, industry and the firm.

iii) Technical analysis appeals mostly to short-term traders or speculators, where as fundamental analysis appeals primarily to long-term investors.

(iii) Efficient Market Theory

The efficient market hypothesis is also called as "Random Walk Theory". It is the extension of fundamental and technical analysis to equity investment decisions. Efficient Market Theory says that no investor can out perform the market for the simple reason that there are numerous knowledgeable analysts and investors who would not allow the market price to deviate from the intrinsic value due to their active buying and selling. Therefore the current market price incorporates all fundamental information. According to William Sharpe "A perfectly efficient market is one in which every security price equalises market value at all times". Eugen Fama expressed that "An efficient capital market is a market that is efficient in processing information". The prices of securities observed at any time are based on "Correct evaluation" of all information available at that time. In an efficient market, prices fully reflect all available information.

The efficient market theory has the following three forms of efficiency:

(a) Weak-form of efficiency

Prices reflect all information found in the record of past prices and volumes.

(b) Semi-strong-form of efficiency

Prices reflect not only all information found in the records of past prices and volumes but also all other publicity available information.

(c) Strong-form of efficiency

Prices reflect all available information, public as well as private.

All the above approaches will be discussed in details in the forthcoming lessons.

1.6 Summary

Security analysis refers to the analysis of trading securities. It analyses the share prices, returns and the risk involved in a security. Every investment is risky and the expected return is related to the risk. The basic purpose of the securities analysis is to find out the intrinsic value of a security for decision making.

Generally the investors have many motives for investing. The investors interest is to earn a better return on their investment by maximising the risk.

There are three approaches in the security analysis to find the real value or intrinsic value of the security. These are:

1) Fundamental Analysis
2) Technical Analysis
3) Efficient Market Hypothesis.

1.7 Key Words

Investment : Investment is the process of purchase of an asset that offers the expectation of income and capital gains.

Security Analysis	:	Security analysis refers to the analysis of trading securities.
Risk	:	Variability of returns associated with a security.
Systematic Risk	:	The systematic risk affects the overall market. The market can be influenced by the nations economy tax reforms or change in the energy situation.
Unsystematic Risk	:	Unsystematic Risk effects a particulars company or industry.
Financial Risk	:	Financial Risk is related with the use of debt financing by companies.
Return	:	Return is the reward to the investor.
Intrinsic Value	:	Intrinsic Value is equal to the present value of a stream of cash flows expected to be generated by the financial asset.

1.8 Questions

1. What is a Security Analysis? What are its objectives?
2. What is the need for Securities Analysis?
3. What is an Intrinsic Value?
4. Explain the various approaches of Securities Analysis?
5. What is Fundamental Analysis? What are its elements?

1.9 Suggested Readings

1. Hampton, John. J., *Financial Decision Making*, 1977, PHI, New Delhi.
2. L.M. Bhole, *Financial Institutions and Markets*, 1999 TMH, New Delhi.
3. V.A. Avadhani, *Investment Management*, 1999, Himalaya Publishing House, Bombay.
4. Fisher and Jordan, *Securities Analysis and Portfolio Management*, PHI, New Delhi.

2

FUNDAMENTAL ANALYSIS

OBJECTIVES

Objectives of this lesson are to:

- explain the concept of fundamental analysis and its importance for investment decision.
- highlight a framework of analysis of Economy – Industry – Company.
- discuss the nature of industry analysis by bringing out different stages of its growth.
- bring out the Company Analysis with a view to identify the potential companies to invest.
- discuss the various issues to evaluate different economy and industry related factors.

2.1 Introduction

Investment decisions are the most important factors involving stock market operations. The investment analysis entails arriving at a decision after collection and analysing the relevant information. Every investor intends to maximise return and minimise the risk of his investment. In order to maximise profits both the decisions are equally important. The fundamental analysis is one of the tools to estimate the intrinsic value of a company's share on the basis of financial data. The fundamental analysis studies the company's every aspect relating to sales, production, profits earning per share and dividends paid etc. It also examines the company's financial strength, its managerial talent, calibre, skills, and competence. It also undertakes government policies and economic conditions and other intangible factors. The fundamental analyst estimates the price that the share of a company deserves to command in the market based on their projections of the company's future earnings.

2.2 Concept of Fundamental Analysis

A fundamental analysis is a time honoured, value based approach depending upon a careful assessment of the fundamentals of an economy, industry and company. The fundamental analysis studies the general economic situation, makes an evaluation of an industry and finally does an in depth analysis, both financial and non-financial of the company.

In the fundamental analysis an attempt is made to analyse various fundamentals or basic factors that affect the risk-return of the securities.

In the fundamental analysis the security analyst or prospective investor is primarily interested in analysing factors such as economic influences industry factors and pertinent company information such as product demand, earnings, dividends and management in order to calculate an intrinsic value for the firm's securities. The investor makes an investment by comparing the intrinsic value with the current market price of a security.

The intrinsic value is the present value of future dividends and capital appreciation computed at an appropriate discount rate to reflect the riskiness of the share. The intrinsic value is also known as the fundamental value. Based on the fundamental value the investor will make a decision to buy or sell a share, by comparing the market price of the shares. If the intrinsic value of a share is higher than the market price the share is to be bought before the market corrects its mistake by increasing the price of the security. On the other hand, if the market price is higher than the intrinsic value, sell that security. This is because the price may be reduced once investors realise and start selling such share.

Based on comparing the intrinsic value and market price of the share the following decisions may be taken.

	Intrinsic Value	*Decision*
i)	If intrinsic value is greater than market price – undervalued security	Buy the security
ii)	If the intrinsic value is lower than the market price – over valued security	Sell the security
iii)	If the intrinsic value is equal to the market price	No action

2.3 Fundamental Analysis – A Framework

Fundamental analysis is based on the analysis of the three main ingredients such as economy, industry and company fundamentals. The analyst should take into account all the three constituents which form different but crucial in making investment decision. Thus, the fundamental analysis is a three phase analysis of (a) the economy b) industry and c) the company.

Three Phase Fundamental Analysis

Phase	*Nature of Analysis*	*Purpose*	*Tools and Techniques*
FIRST	Economic Analysis	To assess the general economics situation of national and international	Economic indicators
SECOND	Industry Analysis	To review prevailing conditions with a	Performance indicators, demand and supply position,

(Contd...)

		specific industry audits segments	competition and government policies
THIRD	Company	To analyse the financial and non-financial aspects of a company to determine whether to buy or sell or hold on to the shares of a company	**Non-financial aspect analysis:** The position of promoters, management, and product quality corporate image, location. **Analysis of financial aspects:** Such as EPS, sales, profitability, dividends record asset growth etc.

The three-phase analysis can be graphically depicted with the three concentric circles shown in the following figure:

PHASES OF FUNDAMENTAL ANALYSIS

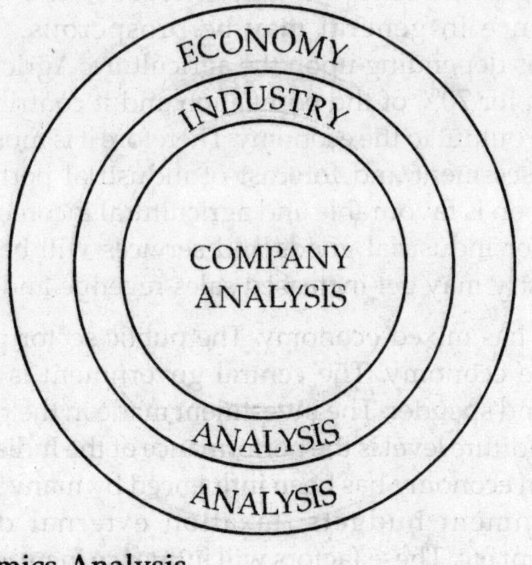

2.4 Economics Analysis

Economic factors play a major role in any investment decision, which is made for making a gain and better return.

Economic analysis and forecasting company performance and of return is necessary for making investments. In the economic analysis the investor has to analyse economic factors to forecast of the economy in order to identify the likely growth of the economy and its trend. Further, the investor will identity those industry groups which are in the coming years and he will be selecting such industry in order to choose the companies in such an industry group. The economic analysis enables the investor to develop a sound economic understanding and be able to interpret the impact of the important economic indicators on stock markets. The economic analysis helps to understand the state of the economy of the country at macro level. The analysis of the state of the economy at macro level incorporates how the economy has performed in the past and how it is performing in the present and how it is expected to perform in the future.

The performance of a company depends on the state of the economy. If the economy is in recession the performance of companies will be bad. If the economy is booming, incomes are rising and demand will increase, the company's performance in general may be prosperous. The Indian economy is depending upon the agriculture. Agriculture is the profession for 70% of the population and it contributes nearly 35% of the output to the economy. Therefore it is most important for the assessment and forecast of industrial performance. If the monsoon is favourable and agricultural income is good the demand for industrial goods and services will be favourable and industry may get increased sales revenue and profits.

India has mixed economy. The public sector plays a vital role in the economy. The central government is the biggest investor and spender. The investment made in the public sector and expenditure level is the performance of the Indian economy. The Indian economy has been influenced by many factors such as government budgets, taxation external debt of the government etc. These factors will influence increased demand and income levels of the public. The changes in taxation policies have an impact on the industry and the corporate sector.

The monetary policy of the government depends on the government's budget policy. The central government borrows money from the public, credit policy of the RBI will show a major impact on the industrial growth. The growth of the industry is mainly depending upon the demand and supply for goods in the country. The monetary and budget policy will influence the price level and interest rates. The interest rates in the free market and the degree of inflation do have a major influence on the economy and the performance of the industries. A low level of inflation is very useful to business sector but higher degree of inflation will dismantle the business plans, lead to escalations and squeeze profit margins. All these factors adversely affect the performance of industry and companies.

The general level of business conditions influences the demand for industrial products and the performance of the industry. The business cycles in the economy may cause fluctuations depending upon the state of the economy. Performance of agriculture sector, availability of energy and other infrastructure outputs imported inputs and other factors. All of these factors do influence the costs and profit margins of the corporate sector.

The economic policies of the government are the most important factor for the Indian economy. The stability of the policies, good performance of the economy in general will influence the company's performance in particular. The stability of the government is the basic foundation for economic policies of the country. The uncertainties in the political system of the country will show greater impact on the economic system. The political uncertainties will show adverse changes in the government policy and also affect the industrial development. The central government policies relating to various projects, foreign direct investment foreign collaborations, foreign investment, price and distribution controls, listing requirements on stock exchanges and other factors do affect the performance of companies. The balance of payment position, the foreign exchange rate may show an impact on the economy and the securities market. All the above factors may influence the economy, which in turn show impact on the corporate sector's performance.

The economic analysis involves the analysing of the following factors:

1. Economic growth
2. Population
3. Monsoon and agricultural production
4. Industrial production
5. Natural resources and availability of raw material
6. Inflation
7. Interest rate
8. Foreign exchange reserves
9. Balance of payment position
10. Budgetary deficit
11. Public debt and foreign debt
12. Domestic savings and capital output rate
13. Employment
14. Taxation policy
15. Infrastructure facilities
16. Government policy
17. Political stability
18. International development
19. Capital formation
20. Savings pattern
21. Research and technological development
22. Economic indicators
23. Economic reforms
24. Foreign direct investment

2.5 Industry Analysis

The second phase of fundament analysis consists of a detailed analysis of specific industry, its characteristics, past record, present state and future prospects. The purpose of the industry analysis is to identify the industries with a potential for future growth and to invest in equity shares of companies selected from such industries. An industry is a homogeneous group of companies. Industry broadly covers all the economic activities happening in a country. A broad concept of industry would include factors of production, transportation, trading activity and public utilities.

The industrial growth of the nation leads to the development of a nation. Industries are to be considered as community interest. Industry consisting of products on process oriented units. They are number of industries. The industries can be divided according to the nature of their function. For ex. Automobile industry, steel industry etc.

The production of commodity is known as manufacturing sector. The manufacturing sector competes with the agriculture, transportation and public utilities. A combination of different industries output, a service sector output is known as Gross National Product (GNP). Each industry is broken down into its logical product classes. The growth of an industry begins with a major technological change. The change in technology results in rapid industrial growth.

The growth of many industries trends to reduce the impact of cost reduction. The cost reduction tends to limit the continued growth of a market. The technological innovation can reduce cost of production substantially. An industry growing at a rapid rate, faster than the national economy will eventually have its growth dampened. A decrease in population growth may lead to a decrease in the rate of growth of industrial sector.

The growth of many industries is divided into 3 stages. They are as follows:

(i) the pioneering stage

(ii) the expansion stage

(iii) the stagnation stage

(i) The Pioneering Stage

Grodirsky presents the pioneering stage. It is the discovery stage. It is associated with the technological development. In this stage there will be a rapid increase in production. The demand for the product is growing rapidly. In this stage a number of companies enter the market to produce the goods and the market is more competitive. Early entered firms will enjoy the larger profits but as the composition increases the profits will also relatively decrease. This situation makes to force out the less efficient firms. In this stage the price stability is available for a little period of time. Speculators and promoters supply the risk capital during this stage. The heavy competition forces influence some weak companies to acquire by strong companies. Therefore, at the end of the stage only a few efficient companies remain in the industry. The examples for this stage are TV, automobiles, radio, electronic industries etc.

(ii) The Expansion Stage

The expansion stage is another stage in the growth of the industry. In this stage the growth cycle is characterised by an expanding demand for the product. But the rate of growth is less than the pioneering stage. In this stage the prices are very stable and the production is quite encouraging. Competition is very high and a small number of big firms dominate the industry. This situation may lead to mergers and acquisitions. The companies that remain in the industry after pioneering and expansion stage are the strong companies. They are well financed. These companies have strong financial infrastructure and their current financial position is excellent. These companies have a strong divided policy and are able to generate resources internally. These companies will have a strong financial architecture making them independent of the long-term capital markets. The investors can invest funds during this stage and substantial growth potential remains in the industry. Therefore, these companies provide safety and security to the investors for their investments. The large companies have been able to retain a sizeable share of the market. The larger firms will have to maintain its status in the industry. The investors have confidence upon these companies. They will get profit from the investment without loosing the principal amount. This stage of industry growth is referred as the period of maturity.

(iii) The Stagnation Stage

The stagnation stage is the final phase of the growth cycle of industry. In this phase some industries will not have growth at all and the output actually declined. In this stage the industry simply loses its power to expand. If the economy shows economic strength, the growth of an industry in this stage does not keep pace. The industry output falls faster than the decline in the economy. The investors should notice that the transition from the expansion stage to the stagnation stage gradually by the companies. In this stage the demand for the product is reduced by competition from other products that influences the profits of the industry by increasing costs. The demand will be influenced by the various factors for a product in this stage.

The fall in the demand for the product is influenced by the following factors:

(a) Price reduction/High prices

(b) Charges in consumers taste

(c) Government regulations

(d) Automation

(e) Miscellaneous factors

The products, which are available in the market, are selling at high prices. The high labour costs force an industry out of a profitable existence. While the demand for a product is declining, prices must be reduced to keep the product competitive. There will be a change in consumer taster that may automatically lead the fall in demand for that product. For example, the tobacco industry.

The government regulations may be against an industry cause to fall in demand for a product. Price support programmes undertaken by the government will influence the competitive position of an industry. For example, the enactment of wage legislation affects an industry's wage costs and reduces its competitive effectiveness. A change in the methods of depreciation provision on assets affects the economic position of an industry.

Automation can bring the changes that will influence the competitive position of an industry. Automation will cause social problems. Machines display the workers. The computers provide tremendous benefits for the nation and for scientific industries. Mechanisation makes us to be competitive in the global markets. Presently India is transforming into mechanised era, which will create benefits as well as harmful to the nation. The automation must be cost effective. The cost of production of a commodity can be reduced substantially by mechanisation of the industry. At the same time there will be a threat of increasing unemployment problem. For ex: one automated machine replaces 20 workers in fabrication sector. The technological change is not an unmixed blessing. If we want to survive in the digital economy, it is necessary to introduce automation in world markets to counter the strong competition.

The miscellaneous factors are excessive productive capacity and rising prices. The over capacity suggests that the growth of the industry is not keeping pace with the national economy.

All of the above factors are the economic classification of industries. Investment services provide basic information to the industry more closely related to the needs of the business. The investor shall know the industry classification used by the investment services. It is necessary to learn in detail the characteristic problems and practices of each industry. The study of the growth of the industries such as pioneering, expansion and stagnation helps us to reach a solution to the problem of where to invest. All of these factors will tell us about the redeployment of the investment. Generally, the investor should select industries, which are in expansion stage of growth cycle. He must concentrate on these areas. The investor should not invest in industries in the pioneering stage, unless he is prepared to accept speculative risk. Further, ignoring the industries that are in the stagnation stage are advisable. Investors should invest after a careful study of the industries, which have developed a strong competitive position, and little threat of obsolescence. A careful analysis of industries is more important to enter into the stock market.

2.6 Company Analysis

Company analysis is a study of the variables that influence the future of a firm both quantitatively and qualitatively. It is a method of assessing the competitive position of a firm, its earnings and profitability, the efficiency with which it operates its financial position and its future earnings per share. The basic purpose of the company analysis is to know the intrinsic value of a share of a company and which depends on the financial performance of a company over a period of time. The terms which are in the same industry are compared to one another to find out which one is the best performer identify the potential company for investment based on its financial position. The company analysis is the most important factor for investment and entering into the stock market. The following factors will help in analysis of particular scrip.

(a) Marketability

(b) Accounting system

(c) Profitability

(d) Dividend policy

(e) Capital structure

(f) Financial analysis

(g) Operating efficiency

(h) Management capability.

The most important factor for selection of a particular company's share is its marketability. The earnings of the company influence the marketability. The share of the company in the industry, growth and stability of its sales determine the earnings. Company, which has a strong competitive position, will provide more earnings. The sales are also dependent on two other major factors such as the operating efficiency of the company and the input costs.

Accounting system is another important element in analysis of thc company's financial position. There is a chance of faulty interpretation of company earnings due to inconsistent accounting policies. The accounting variations are observed for recording costs, expenses and other items, which may change the earnings to a great extent. The accounting policies may also highly influence the inventory pricing, methods of changing depreciation, tax and non-operating income. All these factors show an impact on corporate earnings.

Profitability is the barometer for measuring a company's performance. Investing in a company's security indicates the right to future earnings of that company. Therefore the investor is interested in earnings stability of the company. Generally, the investors select those companies that have stable and growing sales. There is a strong relationship between sales and earnings. The profitability of the company can be analysed with the help of gross profit margin, net profit margin, earning power, return on equity and earning per share ratios. The increasing trend in gross profit margin will indicate the increase in operating income due to a reduction in operating expenses. Net profit margin is the most powerful tool in selecting a particular company's scrip. It is the net profit after tax as percentage of sales. The reduction in corporate tax will enhance the net profit margin and this in turn will influence the intrinsic value of a share. The earning power is the net profit to total assets. Return on equity is the important ratio to determine the per share return. Earnings per share are the ratio of profit after taxes to number of equity shares. It gives the per share earning available to the equity shareholders. Earning per share indicates the amount of surpluses and reserves that the company has generated and retained from its profits over the years.

Dividend policy of the company also influences the value of a share. Some companies will have a stable dividend policy with higher rate of dividend in the future.

Capital structure is another important factor in determining the value of a share. The return on the equity holder's investment can be influenced by financial leverage. The company can use debt funds instead of using total equity funds. The debt equity ratio can be used to analyse the leverage position. A high proportion of preference share capital in the capital structure tends to create thick equity position. The preference shares should be utilised only when it enhances the financial strength and earnings of the company. The debt component in capital structure of the company plays an important role in long-term financing. The debt funds will have lower rate of cost of financing. The interest paid on debt funds is deductible from the profit and reduces the tax liabilities. The use of debt funds due to leverage effect, the equity shareholders earnings may be maximised.

Financial solvency will examine solvency and the liquidity position of the company. The analysis contains a number of parameters. It will enable the company to know about the performance and efficiency of the company in various aspects.

Operating efficiency will reflect the growth of sales volume and increased operating profits. The operating efficiency can be determined from the utilisation of the plant capacity. If the operating efficiency is higher then there will be an increase in earning per share. The future earnings of a company depend upon the ability of the management to invest its funds wisely. The capital expenditure of a company will increase the production capacity in turn the sales.

Management capability is the most important factor in determining the future of the company. The company management should have dynamism, abilities, competency, talent, skills, courage and leadership qualities. Excellent management is paramount to investment success. The quality of the management is the key for successful performance. The ability of the management is the most important element. The management shall have managerial and technical capabilities to run the enterprise efficiently. The management must have the financial capability for the smooth functioning of the production.

Selected Financial Ratios

Ratio analysis is the most important tool available to investors for financial analysis. An accounting ratio shows the relationship in mathematical terms between two interrelated accounting figures. Ratios are used for evaluating the financial conditions and performance of a firm. Ratios can be expressed in two ways, as times and percentage. The ratios can be classified in the following categories:

(i) Profitability ratios
(ii) Liquidity ratios
(iii) Leverage ratios
(iv) Coverage ratios
(v) Activity or turnover ratios.

Equity analysis attaches great importance to the following ratios in financial analysis.

1. *Earnings per share (EPS)*: This indicates after tax profits earned per share. The higher the EPS the better.

$$\text{EPS} = \frac{\text{Profits after tax}}{\text{No. of equity shares}}$$

2. *Price Earning Ratio (P/E ratio)*: This ratio indicates the relationship between market price of the share and earnings per share

$$\text{P/E ratio} = \frac{\text{Market price per share}}{\text{Earnings per share}}$$

3. *Book value per share*: This ratio shows the asset backing available for each share. The higher the book value per share, the better it is for the company.

$$\text{Book value per share} = \frac{\text{Shareholders funds}}{\text{No. of equity shares}}$$

4. *Return on Net worth*: This ratio explains the post tax profits on the shareholders funds. The higher the better.

$$\text{Return on Net worth} = \frac{\text{Profits after tax}}{\text{Shareholders funds}} \times 100$$

5. *Dividend cover*: It denotes the extent to which equity dividends are protected by earnings. The higher the better.

$$\text{Dividend cover} = \frac{\text{Earnings per share}}{\text{Dividend per share}}$$

6. *Profitability of sales*: This indicates the profitability of the sales. The higher is the ratio, better is the profitability.

$$\text{Profitability of sales} = \frac{\text{Profits before tax}}{\text{Sales}} \times 100$$

7. *Debt equity ratio*: Debt as a percentage of equity. The lower the ratio is better.

$$\text{Debt equity ratio} = \frac{\text{Long term debt}}{\text{Shareholders funds}} \times 100$$

2.7 Summary

Investment decisions are the most important. Every

investor intends to maximise return and minimise the risk on his investment. Fundamental analysis is one of the tools to estimate the intrinsic value of a company's share on the basis of financial data. The fundamental analysis helps to study the company's different aspects such as sales, production, profits, earning per share and dividends per share etc. The performance of a company depends on the state of the economy. India has mixed economy. The public sector plays a vital role in the economy. The monetary policy of the government depends on the budget policy. The general level of business conditions influences the demand for industrial products and the performance of the industry. The economic policy of the government is the most important factor for the economy. The fundamental analysis consisting of economic analysis, industry analysis and company analysis. The growth of an industry is divided into three phases such as pioneering stage, expansion stage and stagnation stage. The economic environment may enhance the performance of a company for a period of time. Company analysis helps to select the proposed investment scrip. Ratio analysis is the useful too available to the investors to identify the potential share for investment.

2.8 Key Words

Industry analysis:	Industry analysis is to identify the industries with a potential for future growth and to invest in equity share of companies selected from the industry.
Pioneer stage:	Pioneer stage is the discovery stage of an industry. It is associated with the technological development.
Expansion stage:	Expansion stage of the growth cycle is characterised by an expanding demand for the product.
Stagnation stage :	Stagnation is the final phase of the growth of cycle of an industry. There

	is no pace is production of commodities.
Company analysis:	It is the process of analysing the fundamentals of a company with a view to assesses the prospects for the investment.
Ratio analysis :	Ratio is the relationship between two mathematical figures. It helps to analyse various financial aspects of companies.

2.9 Questions

Essay Questions

1. What is fundamental analysis? Explain the different methods of it.
2. What do you understand by Company Analysis? What are the important parameters to measure the performance of a company?
3. Briefly explain the relevance of Fundamental Analysis in efficient market setup.

Short answer questions

1. Price earnings ratio
2. ROI approach
3. Company analysis
4. Stages of industries
5. Economic indicators
6 Industry analysis.

2.10 Books for Further Reading

Amling F., *Investment – An Introduction to Analysis and Management*, 5th Ed. PHI, New Delhi, 1994.

Francis J.C., *Management of Investment*, 1983.

Donald E. Fischer and Ronald J. Jordon, *Security Analysis and Portfolio Management*, Prentice Hall of India, 1996.

Gangadhar and Ramesh, *Investment Management*, Kalyani Publications, 2002.

Kishan Shah, Pinki Shah and Atul Doshi, *How to Invest Well – A Guide to the Share Market*. Tata McGraw Hill, 1990.

3
TECHNICAL ANALYSIS

OBJECTIVES

The objectives of this lesson are to:

- explain the concept of Technical Analysis.
- pin-point the differences between fundamental analysis and technical analysis.
- highlight the various tools of technical analysis.

3.1 Introduction

The fundamental analysis reveals the intrinsic value of a share. It also explains why the share prices fluctuate. The technical analysis will explain the changes in security prices by studying the market price data. The stock market is different from other markets. The stock market operations will be carried out on a continuous basis. It is involved in buying and selling of the securities. There are many investors who have burnt their fingers by entering the market at the wrong time. The investor shall enter the stock market in bearish environment and exit from the market when bullish environment prevails. Therefore investing time and buying price is the most important factor in winning the success in stock market. The technical analysis is based on notion that all fundamental factors are discounted by the market and are reflected in prices. The share price movement in the share market can be up trend or down trend. The price of a stock depends on supply and demand in the market place. The price is governed by basic economic and psychological inputs. No individual can understand the market price and unable to measure them accurately. The technician can do his guesswork based on important information such as price and volume statistics only.

3.2 Concept of Technical Analysis

The word "Technical" implies a study of market itself and not of the various external factors which affect the market. According to technical analysis, all relevant factors, whatever that may be, get reflected in the volume of the stock exchange transaction and the level of share prices, or more generally to the sum of the statistical information generated by the market. Technical analysis is the study of the market information. The technical analysis is related with the critical study of the daily or weekly price and volume data of the index comprising several shares in the stock market.

The technical analyst does not distinguish between current income and capital gains. The technical analysis does not give great weightage to the intrinsic value of the share. However the analysis depends on the behaviour of stock prices. Further the technical analysis believes that the prices of stock fluctuate based on the demand and supply position in the market. Technical analysis is a simple and useful method to find out the fluctuations of price around the intrinsic value of a share.

3.3 Technical Analysis Vs. Fundamental Analysis

The technical analysis may be used to supplement the fundamental analysis. It confirms findings based on fundamental analysis. Fundamental analysis always the analyst to forecast holding period yield and the risking of achieving that yield. Fundamentalists will hold the securities and expect profits for the long period of holding. The fundamentalist make decisions on quality, intrinsic value and depending on their specific investment goals. Fundamentalists are concerned with the basics, the company's financial strength, and growth in sales, earnings profitability and the investment acceptance. They take into consideration general business and market conditions. The fundamentalists select quality stocks when they are undervalued and sell them when they become fully priced. Technically oriented investors start by checking the market action of the stock. If it is favourable they examine the fundamentals to be sure that the company is profitable and sound. They focus is on the market the performance of all listed scrip. They mainly select the scrip based on price/volume movements of the scrip in the market. The technicians have a strong belief that the stock market prices are influenced to the extent of 15% by the economics and 85% by psychology.

The record of past and present performance of scrip is the key factor. The institutional investors dominate the stock market. The stock market performs on the basis of "follow the leader". The market will tune to the dance of the major money managers. If they start to buy, without any reason the price of the scrip will go up and when they start to sell, it will go down. The technical analysis gives more importance to "volume". Volume is favourable if the number of shares traded is large. The volume is downside if the number of shares traded is small.

The technical analyst recognises that a change in real value is based on the investor's expectations, hopes, fears and industry developments. They are not impressed with fundamental value of scrip. They are with the current and prospective values reflected by market action. The technicians never let sentiment or emotion. They always get out of situation if they are no longer profitable. The technicians give priority to capital appreciation and dividend amount on the security. The technicians want to keep their money disposal at maximum efficiency. They know that there is no real value to any stock and that price reflects supply and demand, which are governed by number of factors rational and irrational.

3.4. Assumptions of Technical Analysis

The technical analysis is based on the following assumptions:

(i) The individual scrip act likes a barometer. A small event is usually discounted in advance with price movements.

(ii) The market price is determined mainly by interaction of demand and supply of security.

(iii) There are both rational and irrational factors, which surround the share supply and demand.

(iv) Change in trends is caused by shifts in the demand and supply position shares.

(v) An upturned in prices of scrip denotes a balance buying, a down trend is an indicative of extreme supply, analysis is the technicians main challenge.

(vi) The upward or downward trend of prices of stocks in the market depends up on the sentiment, psychology and emotions of operators or traders.

(vii) Some chart patterns trend to repeat them.

(viii) The present trends are influenced by the past trends.

3.5. Principles of Technical Analysis

Technical analysis is a science of recording price trends. The stock market prices are recorded in terms of price changes, moving average of prices velocity of price changes, oscillators and the volume of transactions in any scrip together.

The principles involved in technical analysis can be summarised as follows:

The principle of wave motion and trends leads to various types of price trends the buying and selling activities of the market lead to corrections and rallies. It leads to major up-trend and downtrends. The principles of congestion involving support and resistance time results in a phase of activity. In congestion the continuous pressures of buyers dominate the market, there will be an upward movement of prices. If the sellers predominate, there will be a downward trend in the prices. If the buyers dominate the market it is said to be accumulation. If the sellers are increasing their sales it is known as distribution.

The purchase and sale of securities should be done at right time. The right time is the most important factor in the stock market activities. The fundamental rules in stock market operations are to follow the daily charts of high/low/top/bottoms. If the long-term trend is bullish and price trend is increasing, the advance time must make higher tops and higher bottoms. The investor can enter the market at any time so long as the up-trend is continuing as indicated by the higher tops and bottoms. The best time for buy is when the price is declined by 50% of the higher ever peak achieved or at a level of 50% between the extreme low and extreme high price the shares may be sold when prices rise to the old top levels or near to those levels.

Technical Analysis is based on the following principles:

(i) The demand supply of securities in the market will determine the prices of the securities.

(ii) The demand and supply factors of securities are considered to be the main essence of the change in the security prices.

(iii) Technical analysis is a method of presenting the data of securities prices in market to identify by price trends by depicting them on a chart.

(iv) Charts have a method of predicting the significant price movements project future patterns to determine the future prices.

(v) Various charts are applied to predict price movements.

(vi) Charts are also used to find out the total broad spectrum of the market.

(vii) Charts will determine the individual security prices and show the total market index.

3.6. Techniques of Technical Analysis

The technical analysts use various techniques to measure the supply and demand of shares and forecast their prices. The techniques of technical analysis are presented below:

(i) Daily volumes of Transactions

(ii) Floating Stock

(iii) Price Trends

(iv) Rate of Change Method (ROC)

(v) Japanese Candle Stick Method

(vi) Dow Theory

(vii) Elliot Wave Theory

(viii) Advances and Decline Lines Method

(ix) Relative Strength Index.

(i) Daily Volumes of Transactions

The stock markets dynamic continuous places for buying and selling securities. The volume and daily turnover of the market reflects the business activity and creates liquidity. The stock market quotations are presented in print media and electronic media. They are presented in quotations of open, high, low and close. The changes between open and close or high and low can be considered in points or in percentages to reflect the daily volatility, such fluctuations can be done on weekly, monthly, yearly basis to reflect the general volatility of the market. This indicates the signals to the investor against high volatility in any scrip. The market position can be presented through Bar Chart which can be used to depict the daily variations in the stock market.

(ii) Floating Stock

Securities, which are traded in the stock market, are called floating stock. It is the total number of shares available for trading with the public. The volume of trade is the part of the floating stock. The high proportion affecting volumes to floating stock will create greater liquidity for that security which is to be purchased or sold. The increase in price and volume trends is the indicators of the bullish market.

(iii) Price Trends

Technical analysis is a study of the market prices data. The study involves factors affecting supply and demand schedules, prices, volume of trading etc. The study of price and volume trends can be made through the following:

(a) The chartist method

(b) Moving average method

(a) Chartist Method

Generally the technicians depend mostly upon charts of prices and volumes for the analysis of the prices in the market. A chart consists of a base line (horizontal) on which dates are marked. A perpendicular line at right angles to the base line is drawn and prices are marked on it. The chart analysis will reveal the probable strength of demand and pressure of supply at various price levels of the individual stock. The chart enables us to predict the direction in which a stock will move. It also indicates the maximum probable price. Showing the past performance of the stock on the chart along with the current price movement can facilitate the comparison. In the stock market it is assumed that the history always repeats itself. Technicians tell that stock price fluctuations are generally from characteristic pattern. There are countless chart systems but most of them attempt to correlate market price action and the volume of trading. There will be a sign of strength when a scrip advances on a large volume of scrip traded. The chartist method reveals not only the stock behaviour but also its direction. There are three basic types of charts, which are presented below:

(i) Line chart

(ii) Bar chart

(iii) Point chart

i) *Line chart*: on a line chart the closing prices are connected by straight lines. The lines are not specified by the high and low prices of stock for each period.

ii) *Bar chart*: A bar is formed by joining the highest price and the lowest price of a particular share by a vertical line. The closing price of the day is marked by a horizontal mark on this vertical line. Most investors to know the stock price movement for a time period link bar chart. The bar charts are meaningful technique to analyse the share price movements. Bar charts reflect future price trends. The bar charts are very easy to draw. The bar chart preparation prices are very simple. The prices are presented on a graph with a series of vertical lines and each line represents the price movement for a specific time period i.e. a day, a week or even a year. The vertical dimensions of the line represent price, the horizontal dimensions indicate the time period. For eg: In a daily charts each vertical line represents the range of each days activity.

iii) *Point chart*: point chart is the one of the charts used by technicians. The point charts are based on the average prices or closing prices of shares. They are one-dimensional, they only indicate the price changes. Since the points on graph are marked with the figure i.e. the share price, these charts are called point charts. In preparation of the point charts the daily closing share prices are posted in square one above the another, depending on the direction of the price movement. So long as the movement continue in one direction the same column is used. In the point chart each square represents the unit of price and an entry is made on the chart only when the share moves up or down by that specified amount. The following rules apply for preparation of point chart.'

(i) Each column must have at-least two entries.

(ii) Columns alter only when the direction of the price movement changes.

(iii) All intermediate points are marked in transition from one price to another, whether within the same column or in the next one. The point chart analyst gives prominence to the usefulness of the time and volume factors in the stock market. They argue that the prediction of future price fluctuations is based on the analysis of price changes in the stock market.

(b) Moving Average Method

An average is the sum of price of a share over some weekly periods divided by the number of weeks. This point is marked on the latest date for where a price bar has been plotted. This process is repeated for the previous data. The point thus obtained are connected together to give the moving average line. A moving average is a simple presentation of historical data. The data relating is the most important element in moving average. The each data point is the arithmetic average of the previous data. A 15-day's moving average measures the average over the previous 15 days trading.

(iv) Rate of Change Method

This method is useful to indicate more clearly the buy and sell signals. It indicates the rate of change of the price as compared to the price for a certain period back. It can be expressed in percentage of positive or negative. It can be calculated by the following formula.

$$\text{Rate of change (prices/values)} = \frac{\text{Today's price of the scrip}}{\text{Five days back price}}$$

Rate of change depicts the speed upward or downward movements of the price a head of price movement. When the ROC line is above the zero line, the price is rising and when it is below the zero line, the price is falling upside crossing indicating buying opportunities and downside crossing warn you to sell.

(v) Japanese Candlestick Method

It is an enhanced version of a bar chart. It begins to appear in the United States in Mid 1980s. This method will reveal any changes in trends in the short term. It shows scrip open, close, high and low in a three-dimensional format. The three main types are as follows:

(a) Closing price is higher than opening price

(b) Closing price is lower than opening price

(c) Opening and closing prices at the same level or equal

(vi) Dow Theory

The technical analysis evolved 1900-1992 when Charles H. Dow presented the celebrated "Dow Theory". Charles Dow proposed this theory. It is one of the oldest technical analysis methods and still widely followed. This theory has evolved technical approach to the stock market. This theory is built upon the measurement of stock price trends. The Dow theory is based on the movement of the Dow Jones industrial average (DJTA), these two averages are most widely used stock price indices in the USA.

The Assumptions of Dow Theory

The Dow theory is based on the following assumptions:

(i) The averages discount everything.

(ii) The market has the three movements –the primary, secondary and minor movement.

(iii) Price bar charts indicate movement.

(iv) Price/volume relationship provide background.

(v) Price action determines the trend.

(vi) The average must confirm.

The movement of the share prices on the stock exchange has been classified into three major categories.

(i) Primary movements

(ii) Secondary movement

(iii) Daily movement.

(a) Primary Movement

The primary movement of share prices represents the long-term movements. In the primary movement the share prices of one year to three years are more will be studied. If the market price shown a rising trend this situation is known as "Bull phase". If the market prices show a falling trend them it is known as "Bear phase". In bull phase, the bulls dominate the market, then it is called as bullish market. In bullish market, there will be more demand for shares than supply. All the investors will enter the market for procuring shares. The share prices will rise in the stock exchange due to heavy demand for shares. In bearish market the security prices will decline and is dominated by the bears. When all bear operators enter the market, there will be more supply of scrip than demand. When the share prices are declining the investors will force the uncertainty of market situation and dump their holdings in the market. Therefore, the share prices will further decline automatically.

(b) Secondary Movement

The secondary movement represents the study of share prices from 3 weeks to 3 months. It is the study of share prices for short-term period. They are opposite indicator of the primary movements.

(c) Daily Movement

The investors are generally much interested to know the daily price movement of particular scrip before buying that scrip. They will analyse the past behaviour of the scrip. This movement will represent daily irregular fluctuations in the stock prices. They are without any trend. These daily fluctuations do not show any trend. They are mainly due to speculative reasons. These fluctuations can only be useful to speculators. The investor should not base his investment decision on the basis of these movements.

Generally the investors shall purchase the securities at a time when the prices are at lowest and sell at a time when the prices reach the higher level. But the investors do not know when the prices have reached higher level and lower level. Therefore, he should be in a position to identify accurately lower and higher levels of prices. This is technically termed, as identification of the "turn" in the stock exchange price identification of the turn is a difficult task.

There are several problems with this theory. It is not a theory but an interpretation of known data. It does not predict the future stock prices. There are considerable changes between actual and prediction. This theory is a time-tested method of reading the stock market barometer. It will work only when along, wide upward or downward movement is occurred in the stock market. It is mostly unsuitable as a predictor. It does not attempt to explain a consistent pattern of the stock price movements.

(vii) Elliot Wave Theory

R.N. Elliott suggested Elliot Wave principle in 1930. It was popularised by Hamilton Boltan. It attempts to develop a rational for a long-term pattern in the price movements. It states that the major moves take place in five steps. In a bull market the first move is upward, the second is downward, the third phase upward. The waves have a reverse flow in a bear market. It is a valuable tool for market prediction. It offers investors a basis for developing important market strategies. It has some limitations such as difficult to identify by the turning point of each stage.

(viii) Theory of Gaps

The stock market is a continuous market and trading in securities takes place every day except in holidays. A continuous market creates liquidity to the various scrips. The prices are quoted in the stock exchange for listed securities. The differences in the any two days causing discontinuity is known as gap. The higher price of scrip for a day may be lower than the lower price of the previous day, when prices are following the gaps can be categorised in to 4 kinds. Prices move the narrow range, price movement causing for a gap is known as "common gap". The likely to change price trends create a gap in either direction is called as "Break out Gap". If the gaps occur continuously in a downward phase or an upward phase is known as "Runaway" gap. If the gaps occur continuously when the rally is getting exhausted is called as "exhaustion gap".

(ix) Advances Decline lines

A few stocks may be moving ahead while the majority of stocks either making no progress or showing declines. The index relating to advances to decline is known as the advance decline ratio. This ratio will indicate the relative strength of upward or downward movement of prices. If the advances are increasing it is an upward phase and the reverse indicates the downward phase.

(x) Relative Strength Index

It is an oscillator used to discover the inherent strength or weakness of particular scrip. An oscillator is an excellent indicator of over bought /over sold conditions. The relative strength index emphasizes market moves before they occur. The relative strength index tells us whether the net difference between the closing prices is increasing or decreasing. It is calculated for scrip for any number of days such as for 5 or 10 etc. It indicates the strength of price trend. The relative strength index can be calculated by using the following formula:

$$RSI = 100 - \left[\frac{100}{1+RS}\right]$$

$$RS = \frac{\text{Average of 14 weeks up closing prices}}{\text{Average of 14 weeks down closing prices}}$$

This is a powerful indicator and pin points buying and selling opportunities ahead of the market. It ranges in value from 0 to 100. Values above 70 are considered to denote over bought conditions and values below 30 are considered to denote over sold conditions.

3.7 Summary of Technical Analysis

The technical analysis is a science of recording in a graphic form the price trends. Investing time and buying price is the most important factors in winning the success in stock market. The stock prices are governed by basic economic and psychological inputs. The technician can do his guesswork based on only important information such as price and volume statistics. The technical analyst will use the techniques such as daily volumes of transactions, floating stock, price trends, ROC Method, Japanese Candle Stick Method, Dow Theory, Elliot Wave Theory, Theory of Gaps, Advances Decline Ratio, Relative Strength Index.

The stock market quotations are presented in print media and electronic media. They are presented in open, high, low and close. The actively traded stock on bourses is known as floating stock. The price trend can be studied by two methods such as chartist and moving overage method. The ROC Method is useful to indicate more clearly, the buy and sell signals. It can be expressed as percentage and may be positive or negative. Candlestick is an enhanced version of bar chart. Dow Theory explains share price movements in the stock market Elliot wave Theory attempts to explain long-term pattern in the price movements. The theory of Gaps reveals the gap in prices of only two days.

3.8 Key Words

Technical Analysis	: The technical analysis will explain the changes in security prices. It is the study of the stock market information.
Floating Stock	: The most actively traded scrip on the bourses.
Chartist Method	: The chart reveals the demand and supply of share prices at various price levels on the individual stock.
Bull Phase	: When the share prices show a rising trend is known as bull phase in the market.
Roc Method	: The rate of change reveals the buy and sell signals.
Dow Theory	: It is the oldest technical method still widely followed to study the movement of share prices.

3.9 Questions

Essay Questions

1. Briefly describe the essence of technical analysis.
2. Explain the differences between fundamental and technical analysis.
3. Explain the statement "The stock market acts like a barometer rather than a thermometer".
4. Discuss in detail the Dow Theory and how it will be used to determine the direction to the stock market.
5. Critically examine the Elliot Wave principle for stock market price prediction.

6. Compare and contrast point charting and bar charting.

Short Questions

1. What is a technical analysis?
2. What is a Dow Theory?
3. What is charting?
4. What is moving average method?
5. What is relative strength index?
6. How rate of change is useful for price prediction?
7. What is a chart?
8. What is a price bar chart?
9. What are the principles of technical analysis?

3.10 Suggested Readings

1. V.K.Bhalla, *Investment Management*, S. Chand & Co. Ltd., 1999.
2. S.N. Maheshwari, *Financial Management: Principles and Practice*, S. Chand & Sons.
3. V.A. Avadhani, *Investment Management*, Himalaya Publishing House, Bombay.
4. Donald E. Fischer and Ronald J. Jordan, *Security Analysis and Port Folio Management*, Prentice Hall of India, New Delhi.
5. P. Clifford, *Technical Analysis*, Vision Books. New Delhi, 1992.
6. Martin J., *Technical Analysis*, McGraw Hill, New Delhi, 1985.

4

EFFICIENT MARKET THEORY

OBJECTIVES

The objectives of this lesson are to:

- explain the concept of Efficient Market Theory.
- study the price changes in market through various methods.
- highlight the challenges before security analysis.

4.1 Introduction

The efficient market hypothesis otherwise known as the Random Walk Model is the logical extension of the fundamental and technical analysis for equity investment decisions. The Efficient Market Hypotheses (EMH) considers that individuals cannot out perform the market for the simple reason that, there are numerous knowledgeable analysts and investors who would not allow the market price to deviate from the intrinsic value due to their active buying and selling. It is also observed that the current market price will reflect the intrinsic value and therefore, there is no need for fundamental or technical analysis.

The information known to the public is immediately discounted by all inverters and will be reflected in share prices in the stock market. All investors know the all-possible information and behave rationally. The price changes will be influenced by new information and stock prices will automatically adjusted accordingly. The securities markets are said to be efficient if the following conditions are satisfied:

(a) Transaction costs are ignored.

(b) Every investor is freely allowed to borrow or lend at the same rate.

4.2 Definition of Market Efficiency

Eugene Fama states that "An efficient capital market is a market that is efficient in processing information. The prices of securities observed at any time are based on correct evaluation of all information available at that time in an efficient market prices fully reflect all available information".

William Sharpe stated that "A perfectly efficient market is one in which every security price equals its market value all times".

The Random Walk Theory points out that the financial markets are so competitive that there is immediate price adjustment. This is because of great communication system through which information can be distributed. The speed at which information spreads will determine the efficiency of the market. According to the theory that the changes in prices of stocks show independent behaviour and are dependent on the new piece of information that are received but with in themselves are independent of each other.

The basic essential fact of Random Walk Theory is that the information on stock prices is immediately and fully spread so that other investors have full knowledge of the information.

4.3 Assumption of EMH

The Random Walk Theory is based on the following assumptions.

(a) The share prices of the market discount all the available information quickly.

(b) The flow of information is free and unbiased therefore the markets are efficient.

(c) Every investor has free access to the same information and no one has superior knowledge.

(d) The stock market is wide and it is supreme, no individual investor or group of individuals can influence the market.

(e) The supply and demand of the shares is free and the markets can quickly adjust it.

(f) The information relating to the fundamentals will influence the market price.

(g) The share prices will move in an independent manner.

(h) No individual has inside information.

(i) The demand and supply forces for a share are the result of rational investment decisions.

(j) Institutional investors or any major fund managers cannot influence the stock market.

4.4 Forms of Efficient Market Theory

The information available to the public can be categorised into three forms. The past prices, other public information and inside information. These factors may be used to make average returns on investment. In an efficient market if an investor he will earn above average return knows the information otherwise he may be involved in risk. The market efficiency can be classified as follows:

(a) Weak form (Price information)

(b) Semi strong form (Other public information)

(c) Strong form (Inside information).

A) Weak Form

Weak Form is the oldest technique of the efficient market theory. According to this method, the stock market price reflects all known information with reference to part stock prices, trends and volumes. This theory reveals that past data cannot be used to predict future stock price. This theory is also popularly known as Random Walk Theory. It reveals that the price changes are independent. The prices of the stock market at any time will on the average reflect the intrinsic value of the security the trends provide no basis for forecasting the future. The statistical investigations to provide support for the weak form of the efficient market hypothesis are presented below:

(a) Filter Rules

(b) Correlation

(c) Run Test

(a) According to filter rules if a stock moves up to a 5% level then buy that share and hold it. If the share price declines up to 5% sell it and take a short position. Short position is a situation where one sells even without holding shares to deliver. Filtering is the screening of the important information affecting the share prices from lots of unimportant data. Fama, Blume and Alexander conducted these tests. Their tests did not give conclusive proofs. Generally a filter level varying from 0.5% to 5%.

(b) Serial correlation is used to measure the one series of security prices with a series in the past. It measures the correlation coefficient of price changes of a week that of the price changes in a week later and so on down the line. The price changes of this week do not therefore depend on the past price changes to any significant extent. Fama studied the relationship and found that there is no significant price change in successive periods. This correlation test did not show significant positive results. Therefore the prices move in an independent manner to a large extent.

(c) Run Test is a set of consecutive price changes in the same direction. It has shown that the market was not perfect and that the transaction costs are so high that those trading in the market could not make abnormal returns, most of the studies proved that security prices moved in a random manner and are not amenable to any precise forecast.

B) Semi Strong Form

According to the Semi Strong Form Theory, the market absorbs quickly and efficiently not only the price information but also all publicly available information. The public information is found in the form of financial reports such as balance sheet, profit and loss accounts, and earning and financial results. The other financial elements like financial structure, liquidity, solvency effects, and the profitability of the company. The business related information would also flow in as news affecting the market. Any change in conditions of the company and revision of data effect the share price in the market. Time is the most important element in the stock market operations. The impact of any change of fundamentals on the company share price will be reflected in time lag. The market will discount some events even before its announcement is made. There matters such as earnings bonus issue, rights issue would affect the market even before the formal announcement by the company. These tests are invariably based on pricing models such as economic model or capital asset pricing model. This theory reveals that the absorption of the information on share price was inefficient and differs from a script to script and the time period studied. It is empirically not well supported but in foreign markets it is found to be applicable and market quickly absorbs all published information.

C) Strong Form

Strong Form of efficient market hypothesis is perfect that the market price of shares will be discounted by private information, inside information and unpublished data. Generally, investors whenever they enter in the market can gain average returns. All information contents will not be useful to the market but some superior contents can give better market returns. This analysis is only possible to inside traders, floor brokers and institutional investors. They are having highly efficient market research components. The research studies found that the strong form of efficient market does not exist in developed markets. The common investors have not benefited with all the information available to them. Therefore, the average investor could do better by picking up securities in a random method.

4.5 Challenges to the Securities Analysis

The efficient market hypothesis challenges the traditional security analysis in the following manner:

(a) Challenge to the chartists

(b) Challenge to the fundamental analyst.

The random walk model is a description of reality and the work of the chartist is no real value in stock market analysis. The chartist can use his techniques to make better than chance prediction of stock prices. The chartist consistently use these patterns to do more meaningful predictions of future price.

The stock prices in any time will represent good estimates of intrinsic value of a share of the markets are efficient and the random walk theory is treated as valid. The fundamental analysis cannot be used to provide any additional information to forecast the share prices based on the intrinsic value. Because the stock prices will reflect all possible financial and non-financial information of a share. Therefore, there will not be any role to fundamental analysis to forecast the superior price trends.

4.6 Criticism of Efficient Market Hypothesis

The findings of the various studies vary widely to the efficient market theory. Some accept the efficient market theory in toto, some other rejects it. The criticism of efficient market theory is based on the following:

(a) Perfect Markets

(b) Velocity of the new information

(c) Evaluation of information.

(a) Perfect Markets

The efficient market theory reveals that at any time the stocks will reflect the intrinsic value of the shares. The entering, exit time is the most important in the stock market operations. But some time the stocks are not priced on estimates of actual value. The efficient market theory assumes that the markets are more perfect. Generally, it is very difficult to find perfect markets due to the influence of the various factors.

(b) Velocity of the New Information

It is also felt that news of the business is freely available to all the investors. The efficient market theory suggests that news does not flow instantaneously. It implies that no one can have the monopolistic power over the market. The stock recommendations based on unfounded beliefs. The brokerage firms and investment firms are specialised in research activities and they have enormous power in the market and can direct tremendous money flows in and out of stocks. Speculators are interrelated to buy and sell the shares for a short period to gain the market advantages. Many speculators may buy and sell a stock because they believe that an influential brokerage house may recommend that script.

(c) Evaluation of Information

The value of a script will be reflected after discounting the new information. The experience of the security analyst can convert the information into specific estimates of true value. There is a considerable scope for a financial manager to use his intellectual abilities to investment performance.

4.7 Efficient Market Theory: Summary

All the relevant information is reflected in the current stock prices. The price changes will be influenced by new information. The information, which is available to the public, can be categorised into three kinds. The past prices, other public information and other side information. They are further known as weak form semi-strong form and strong form. The weak form is the oldest method in efficient market theory. It reveals that the price reflects all known information with reference to past stock prices, trends and volumes. The weak form consists of filter rules correlation and run test.

Semi strong form reveals that the market absorbs quickly and efficiently not only the price information but all publicity available information. The publicity available information is in the form of financial reports such as balance sheet, profit and loss accounts earnings and financial results. It is empirically not well supported but in developed markets it is found to be applicable. The market quickly absorbs all published information.

According to strong form of EMH that the market prices of shares will be discounted by private information, insider information and unpublished data. All information contents will not be useful to the market, but some superior and qualitative information can give better returns.

4.8 Questions

1. Define the efficient market hypothesis.
2. What is the role of new information in the pricing of securities
3. Distinguish among three forms of market efficiency
4. Define market efficiency
5. Describe the different tests of weak form of EMH
6. What are the limitations of EMH?
7. What are the implications of EMH for technical analysis?

4.9 Suggested Readings

1. V.K. Bhalla, *Investment Management*, S. Chand & Co. Ltd.
2. V.A. Avadhani, *Investment Management*, Himalaya Publishing House, Bombay.
3. E. Fama, Efficient Capital Markets: A Review of Theory and Empirical Work, *Journal of Finance*, May, 1970.
4. Fisher and Jordan, *Securities Analysis and Portfolio Management*, PHI, New Delhi.

5

PORTFOLIO ANALYSIS AND MANAGEMENT

OBJECTIVES

The objectives of this lesson are to:

- explain the concept of portfolio and need for portfolio
- highlight the concept of diversification of risk
- discuss the portfolio process.

5.1 Introduction

Investment is the employment of funds with the aim of achieving additional income or growth in value. It is aimed at earning return in the future. It involves the commitment of resources, which have been saved or put away from current consumption of resources in the hope that some benefits will accrue in future. Whereas, portfolio analysis builds on the estimates of future returns and risk of holding various combination of assets. As we know, individual assets have risk return characteristics of their own. Portfolio's on the other hand, may or may not take on the aggregate characteristics of their individual parts.

5.2 Concept of Portfolio

Portfolio is the collection of financial or real assets such as equity shares, debentures, bonds, treasury bills and property etc. In a more general sense the term portfolio may be used synonymous with the expression "collection of Assets" which can even include physical assets (gold, silver, real estate etc.,) Portfolio means a collection or combination of financial assets (securities) such as shares, debentures and government securities. Portfolios are combination of assets. Portfolio will consist of collection of securities. What is to be borne in mind is that, in the portfolio context, assets are held for investment purposes and not for consumption purposes. These holdings are the result of individual preferences and decisions of the holders regarding risk and return and a host of other considerations.

Portfolio management is the investment of funds in different securities in which the total risk of the portfolio is minimised while expecting maximum return from it. Portfolio management takes the ingredients of risk and returns for individual securities and considers the mixing of these securities. The portfolio management in total includes the planning, supervision, forming rationalism and conservatism involved in the selection of securities to meet investor's objectives. It entails choosing the one best portfolio to suit the risk-return preferences of the investors. It also encompasses the evaluation and revising the portfolio in view of changing risk, return and investors risk preferences.

5.3 Need for Portfolio

The portfolio is needed for the selection of optimal, portfolio by rational risk averse investors i.e. by investors who attempt to maximise their expected return consistent with individually acceptable portfolio risk. Portfolio is essential for portfolio construction. The portfolio construction refers to the allocation of funds among a variety of financial assets open for investment. Portfolio concerns itself with the principles governing such allocation. The objective of the portfolio theory is to elaborate the principles in which the risk can be minimised, subject to the desired level of return on the portfolio or maximise the return, subject to the constraint of a tolerable level of risk. The need for portfolio management arises due to the objectives of the investor. The emphasis of portfolio management varies from investor to investor. Some want income, some capital gains and some combination of both. However, the portfolio analysis enables the investors to identify the potential securities, which will maximise the following objectives:

Security of the principal, stability of income, capital growth, marketability, liquidity and diversification.

Thus the basic need of the portfolio is to maximise yield and minimise the risk. The other ancillary needs are as follows:

1. Providing regular or stable income.
2. Creating safety of investment and capital appreciation.
3. Providing marketability and liquidity
4. Minimising the tax liability

5.4 Portfolio Process

Portfolio Management is a process encompassing many activities of investment in assets and securities. It is a dynamic and flexible concept and involves continuous and systematic analysis, judgement and operations. The portfolio process involves the steps such as investment policy, investment analysis, and valuation of securities and construction of optimal portfolio, which will minimise the overall risk and maximise the return. In the process of portfolio, firstly, it involves construction of a portfolio based upon the fact of the investor's objectives, constraints, preference for risk and return and his tax liability. Secondly, the portfolio is reviewed and adjusted from time to time with the market conditions. The adjustment is done through changes in the weighting pattern of the securities and asset classes in the portfolio. The shifting of assets and securities will take advantage of changes in market conditions and in prices in the securities and assets in the portfolio. Thirdly, the evaluation of portfolio performance is to be done by the manager in terms of targets set far risk and return and changes in the portfolio are to be affected to meet the changing conditions.

5.5 Traditional Views

Since 1950s, a body of knowledge has been built up which quantifies the expected return and risk of the portfolio. These studies have come to be know as portfolio theory. Thus portfolio theory has been developed to provide the management with which it can evaluate the merits of an investment portfolio and thereby select the most efficient portfolio which will provide the best trade off between risk and return.

The traditional portfolio analysis has been a very subjective nature but it has provided success to the investors who have made their investment by making analysis of individual securities through evaluation of return and risk conditions in each security. According to this theory there was a possibility of getting maximum return at the minimum risk or achieve expected return at a low risk. The traditional theory of portfolio management is based on the fact that risk could be measured on each individual security through the process of finding out the standard deviation and security should be chosen where the standard deviation was lowest. Greater variability and higher deviation showed more risk than those securities, which had lower variation. The traditional view believes that the market is in efficient and the fundamental analysis can take the advantage of the situation. In the traditional approach risk is a quantitative variable and actual portfolios are derived intuitively. The traditional approach typically involves two major decisions. These are:

(a) Determining the appropriate portfolio objectives

(b) Selecting the securities to be included in the portfolio

Further, the principal objective of the traditional theory of portfolio management is to maximise the expected utility of the investor. The portfolio selected must supposed to be maximised the investor utility preference for the risk and return. The investor's utility preference for the risk and return. It implies that the investor will attempt to maximise the expected return subject to the level of risk involved.

In constructing investment portfolio to the company's needs and objectives, the management must study investment merits of the total portfolio as a single entity because that would, besides facilitating analysis of the merits of individual securities, study interaction among these securities. The portfolio theory takes cognizance of the sordid fact that the sum of the individual securities merits does not have to equal the attractiveness of the entire portfolio as such.

Accordingly, it provides specific measure, which enables the management to evaluate the investment merits of a portfolio, compare with it with other portfolios and finally, choose the optimal portfolio for the organization. A number of portfolio models, which contain methods for preparing an attractive, efficient frontier and choosing from the frontiers the optimal portfolio have been developed.

5.6 Diversification of Risk

Risk in a portfolio can be reduced by a proper diversification into a number of scrips. The efforts to spread and minimise portfolio risk take the form of diversification. Most investors prefer to held several assets rather than putting all their eggs into one basket, with the hope that if one goes bad, the other will provide some protection from extreme loss. Surely enough there is merit in this approach. Although some investors held a contrary view point that recommends putting all eggs into one basket and then keeping a sharp eye on the basket.

Diversification of one's holdings is intended to reduce risk in an economy in which every asset's returns are subject to some degree of uncertainty. Most investors hope that if they hold several assets, even if one goes bad, the others will provide some protection from an extreme loss. Efforts to spread and minmise risk take the from of different types of securities across industry lines.

The companies chosen should not be too many or too few but of an optimum size as to be efficiently manageable. The economics of scale in management apply to this analysis. It will be illustrated in the following graph, that the higher the risk, higher is the return in normal process.

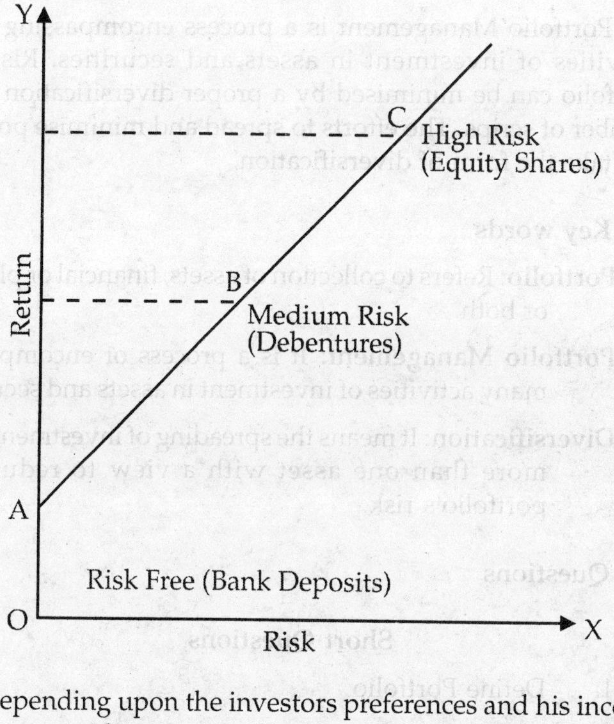

Depending upon the investors preferences and his income requirements, the strategy of investment should be at A, B or C respectively. Assuming that he takes some risk at B or C, this risk can be reduced so far as it concerns the specific company risk, but the market risk is outside the control of the portfolio manager. The risk can be reduced by a proper diversification of scrips invested.

5.7 Summary

Portfolio is the collection of financial or real assets, such as equity shares, debentures, bonds, treasury bills and property etc. In the portfolio context, assets are held for investment purposes and not for consumption purposes. Portfolio management is the investment of funds in such combinations of different securities in which the total risk of the portfolio is minimised while expecting maximum return from it. The portfolio construction refers to the allocation of funds among a variety of financial assets open for investments.

Portfolio Management is a process encompassing many activities of investment in assets and securities. Risk in a portfolio can be minimised by a proper diversification into a number of scrips. The efforts to spread and minimise portfolio risk take the form of diversification.

5.8 Key words

Portfolio: Refers to collection of assets, financial or physical or both.

Portfolio Management: It is a process of encompassing many activities of investment in assets and securities.

Diversification: It means the spreading of investments over more than one asset with a view to reduce the portfolio's risk.

5.9 Questions

Short Questions

1. Define Portfolio
2. What is Portfolio Management?
3. What is portfolio diversification?
4. What is a portfolio process?
5. What is a need for portfolio selection?

5.10 Books for Further Readings

1. Elton, Edwin J. and Grufer, Martin J., *Modern Portfolio Theory And Investment Analysis*, John Wiley & Sons, 1987.

2. Alexander, Gorden J. and Sharpe, William F., *Fundamentals of Investments*, Prentice-Hall.

3. V.A. Avadhani, *Investment and Securities Markets in India*, Himalaya publishing.

6
PORTFOLIO SELECTION

OBJECTIVES

The objectives of this lesson are to:

- discuss the Portfolio Section Problems and Process
- illustrate the Markowitz Approach
- identify the Efficient Portfolio
- explain the Construction of Optimum Portfolio.

6.1 Introduction

The determination and selection of a multi security portfolio is complicated affair as there are possibility of infinite number of combinations of various securities that can enter a portfolio. The securities available to an investor can be combined in any proportion and hence any number of portfolios can be built. Each such portfolio can be described in terms of its expected rate of return and the risk. Thus, this unit has provided some insights into models for portfolio selection to trace the efficient set.

6.2 Models for Portfolio Selection

The identification and selection of an efficient portfolio is a complicated job. An investor must select a portfolio which will best suit his requirements, out of all those available to him.

The following two are the most popular models for portfolio selection.

1. Markowitz Model.
2. Capital Asset Pricing Model.

6.3 Markowitz Theory of Portfolio Management

According to Markowitz, the portfolio theory establishes a relationship between a portfolio's expected return and its level of risk as the criterion for selecting the optimum portfolio.

Thus two measures were suggested for evaluating the merits of a portfolio, i.e.

1. The expected return from the portfolio and
2. The level of risk exposure associated with the portfolio.

The risk is the statistical notion of variation or standard deviation of return. The Markowitz theory is also based on diversification. It believes in asset correlation and in combining assets the risk can be lowered.

Assumptions of Markowitz Theory

The Markowitz theory of portfolio management is based on the following assumptions:

1. Market is efficient: The market information is freely available to all the players in the market and all the investors have access to the market information. No single investor can make superior profits. All investors in equal category.
2. The investors have common goal: All investors will avoid risk. They are risk average.
3. Investors will expect maximum return.
4. Investors will take the decisions based on the expected rate of return of an investment.
5. The diversification of portfolio will maximise the return and minimise the risk.

6. Investors assume high return for high risk and low return for low risk.
7. Risk can be reduced by diversification of portfolios.
8. An investor can get higher return for each level of risk "by determining the efficient set of securities".

So as to find the efficient set of portfolios and select the most efficient one the portfolio manager will need to know the expected return and the risk of these returns for the various individual securities. Additionally, the covariance between the stocks and all other combination of the remaining stocks will be required. From this, he can compute the expected return and risk of the possible portfolios.

Markowitz approach determines for the investor the efficient set of portfolio through three important variables i.e., return, standard deviation and coefficient of variation. It is also called the "Full co-variance Model". Through this model the investor can find out the efficient set of portfolios by finding out the trade off between risk and return, between the limits of zero and infinity.

According to the theory the effect of one security purchase over the effect of the other security purchase is taken into consideration and results are evaluated.

The expected return on the portfolio, according to Markowitz is the weighted average of the return to each security in the portfolio. This is described notionally as:

$$R_p = \sum_{i=1}^{N} R_i X_i \quad \text{(OR)} \quad R_p = \sum_{i=1}^{N} X_i R_I$$

Where,

R_p = expected return on portfolio.

R_i = expected return to security i.

X_i = the proportion of total portfolio invested in security i.

N = Total number of securities in the portfolio.

For example, assume Rs.1,000 is used to construct a portfolio of four shares A, B, C and D. the money is allocated to the shares in the proportion of 0.1, 0.4, 0.3, and 0.2 respectively. The returns on these securities are 15, 10, 20 and 25 percent respectively. The return on the portfolio would be:

$$R_p = \Sigma R_1X_1 + R_2X_2 + R_3X_3 + R_4X_4$$
$$= 0.15 * 0.1 + 0.10 * 0.4 + 0.20 * 0.3 + 0.25 * 0.2$$
$$= 0.165$$
$$= 16.5\%$$

Alongside the expected return to the portfolio, the portfolio manger must also consider the risk associated with the portfolio. The risk of the portfolio consists of the risk of the individual securities and the covariance between the returns of the securities amongst all possible combinations of them. The risk of a portfolio comprising two shares A and B, can thus be expressed (using variance as the measure of risk):

$$\text{Covariance of AB} = X^2_A\sigma^2_A + X^2_B\sigma^2_B + 2X_AX_Br_{AB}\sigma_A\sigma_B$$

COV.AB = The covariance between the rates of return on shares A and B

Where:

r_{AB} = Coefficient of correlation between A&B shares

σ^2 = Variance of portfolio

X^2_A = Proportion inverted in share A

X^2_A = Proportion inverted in share B

σ^2_A = Variance of the rate of return on share A

σ^2_B = Variance of the rate of return on share B

The term covariance explains the relationship between the movements in the rates of return from shares A and B. it is derived from the following formula

$$COV.AB = r_{AB}\,\sigma_A\,\sigma_B$$

Assume for example, a sum of money is inverted equally in two shares X and Y, which are expected returns of 8 and 6 per cent, respectively. The variance of X and Y is zero (i.e., r=0). The expected return and the portfolio risk would be as given below:

The expected return = $R_x X_x + R_y X_y$

$= (0.8)\,(0.5) + (0.06)(0.5)$

$= (0.04) + (0.03)$

$= 0.07$ or 7%

The portfolio risk = $X_{x2}\sigma^2 + X_{y2}\sigma_{y2} + 2X_x * X_y r_{xy}\sigma_x\sigma_y$

$= (0.25)\,(0.02) + (0.25)\,(0.02) + 2\,(0.5)\,(0.5) \times 0$

$= (0.25)\,(0.02) + (0.25)\,(0.02) + 0$

$= 0.005 + 0.005$

$= 0.01$

By purchasing equal amounts of the two shares, the rates of return of which are not correlated at all, the risk of the portfolio is half that had all the portfolio money been invested in X or Y solely.

Where there are many shares in consideration for inclusion in the portfolio, the covariance of each security with every other security and combination of securities will have to be measured. This will involve enormous and cumbersome computations. In place of these computations Dr. Markowtz established a computer programme.

Markowtz programme involves the complex mathematics of quadratic programming. Because this can be done only with the help of computers his theoretical ideas and their practical application are limited to the most sophisticated investors equipped with computers.

In this connection it should be remembered that if there is perfect positive correlation (r = +1) then there will be no risk reduction by diversification, as long as the proportion X invested in the portfolio is set equal to.

$$= \frac{\sigma X^2}{\sigma x^2 + \sigma y^2}$$

i.e. in the example

$$\sigma^2 = (0.25)(0.02) + (0.25)(0.02) + 2(0.5)(0.5)\ 1$$
$$= (0.005) + (0.005) + (0.5)\ 1\ (0.02)$$
$$= 0.01 + 0.01$$
$$= 0.02 \text{ or } 2\%$$

This is the same as the individual variances on shares X and Y. If the correlation coefficient is perfectly negative (r = 1) then there will be no portfolio risks again, as long as the proportion X, invested in the portfolio is equivalent to

$$= \frac{\sigma X^2}{\sigma x^2 + \sigma y^2}$$

$$\text{i.e } \sigma^2 = (0.25)(0.02) + (0.25)(0.02) + 2(0.5)(0.5)(-1)(X)$$
$$= (0.005) + (0.005) + (0.5)(-1)(0.02)$$
$$= 0.01 - 0.01$$
$$= 0$$

So long as the correlation between rates of return of share is less than +1, combining them will reduce the variance of the portfolio and the near the correlation is to –1, the less the risk will be.

6.4 Dominance Principle

The dominance principle has been developed in the portfolio selection to understand the risk return trade-off conceptually. As in efficient frontier analysis, it is assumed that inverters prefer returns and dislikes risks. It may be observed from the following figure:

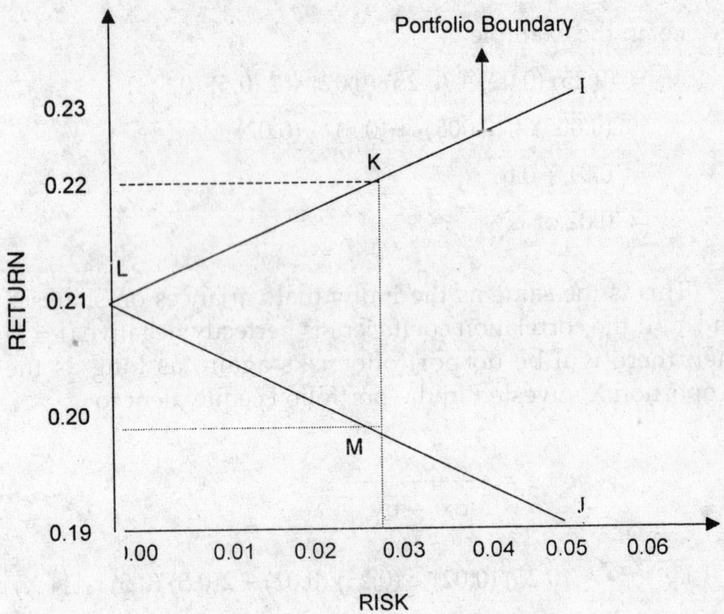

According to the above graph, if an individual experience the higher expected return with portfolio 'K', than with portfolio 'M' but the risk associated with both the portfolio is the same. He would prefer portfolio 'K' because it dominates portfolio "M". In fact all the portfolios lying along the lower part of the dot-line are dominated by portfolio's laying along upper part. Portfolio that lie along the boundary between points I and L are therefore, termed as efficient in that each represented the maximum expected return for a given level of risk. The points K and M are directly comparable because they have a common standard deviation. It is difficult to say risk versus return compare with the other portfolios, because the risk and return are not directly comparable using the dominance principle, the portfolios without the common risk or returns factors are not directly comparable.

6.5 Feasible Set

Investment in risk free asset is often referred to as risk free lending. If the investor purchases this asset at the beginning of the holding period, then the investor knows exactly what the value of the asset will be at the end of the holding period. With the introduction of a risk free asset, the investor is now able to put part of his money in this asset and the remaining in any of the risky portfolio's that are in Markowitz's "feasible set". Adding there new opportunities expands the feasible set significantly and more importantly, changes the location of part of Markowitz's efficient set. The nature of these changes needs to be analysed since investors are concerned with selecting a portfolio from the efficient set. In doing so, consideration is given initially in determining the expected return and standard deviation for a portfolio that consists of combining an investment in the risk free asset an investment in a single risky security.

6.6 Efficient Frontier

Efficient frontier is the set of portfolios of a given population of assets, which offer the maximum possible expected return for a given level of risk. The portfolio manager selects his portfolio from the efficient portfolios. Efficient portfolios are those portfolios, which from among all the attainable portfolios offer the highest return at a particular level of risk or minimum risk for given level of return.

On the basis of expected return and risk and covariance analysis the portfolio manager picks up securities from the available securities and constructs a portfolio. Since, there may be several combinations of securities based on expected return and risk, attainable set of portfolios emerge. For example, the following may be the possible portfolio expected from returns and risks.

Portfolio	*Expected Return (Per cent)*	*Risk*
A	15	13
B	13	8
C	10	4
D	8	3
E	5	4
F	5	9
G	10	12
H	10	12
I	7	8
J	9	7

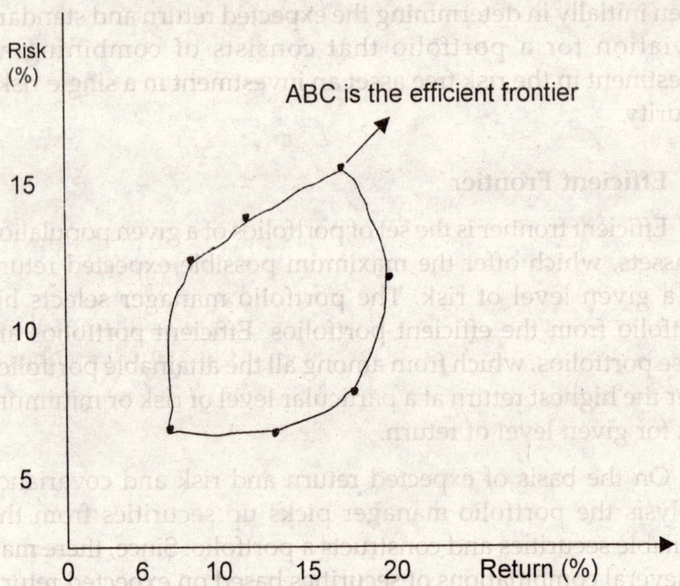

Each of the portfolios along or within line ABCEDFG is possible. There can not be any portfolio outside of this perimeter because no combination of expected return and risk exists there.

Among the various possible portfolios some are more attractive than others. Thus, for example, portfolio 'C' is more appealing than the portfolio H or G because C offers the same returns as the other two but at a lower risk exposure as revealed by standard deviation. Similarly, portfolio H is more attractive than portfolio F, because H offers a high return for the same level of a risk exposure.

The general rule for identifying attractive portfolio is that any portfolio offering a higher returns for the same level of risk or a lower risk exposure for the same return than another portfolio will be considered more attractive than the other portfolio. From the attractive portfolios the manager will choose some portfolios that offer the highest return at a particular level of risk. The portfolios thus selected are designated as efficient portfolios.

6.7 Construction of Optimum Portfolio

Construction of optimum portfolio refers to the allocation of funds among a variety of financial assets open for investment. Portfolio theory concerns itself with the principles governing such allocation. The objective of the theory is to elaborate the principles in which the risk can be minimised, subject to a desired level of return on the portfolio or maximise the return subject to the constraint of a tolerable level of risk.

Therefore, the construction of an optimum portfolio is to maximise yield and minimise risk. The other ancillary objectives are as follows:

1. Regular income or stable return
2. Appreciation of capital
3. Marketability and liquidity
4. Safety of investment
5. Minimising tax liability

The persuasion of these objectives, the portfolio manager has to construct the optimum portfolio with their projected return and risk and choose only those investments, which satisfy the requirements of the individual investor can cater to his preferences.

6.8 Capital Asset Pricing Model

The Capital Asset Pricing Model (CAPM) attempts to measure the risk of a security in the portfolio. It considers the required rate of return of a security on the basis of its contribution to total portfolio risk. It provides that in a well-functioning efficient market, the risk premium varies in direct proportion to risk. It also provides a measure of risk premium and a method of estimating market risk-return line. The risk of a well-diversified portfolio depends on the market risk of the securities included in the portfolio. The market risk of a security is measured in terms of its sensitivity to market movements. The core idea of the CAPM is that only nondiversifiable risk is relevant to the determination of expected return on any asset. Since the diversification risk can be eliminated, there is no reward for it. In fact, the CAPM can be used to examine the risk and return of any type of capital asset such as individual security, an investment project or a portfolio of assets/ investment. However, for the time being, the CAPM is being discussed here with reference to risk and return of a security only.

The CAPM is based on the following assumptions:

1. The investors are basically risk averse and diversification is needed to reduce the risk.
2. All investors have identical estimates of risk and return of all securities.
3. All investors can borrow or lend an unlimited amount of funds at risk free rate of interest.
4. All investors want to maximise the wealth and the portfolio selection is on the basis of risk and return assessment.

5. All investments are efficiently diversified and have eliminated the unsystematic risk.
6. All the securities are perfectly divisible and liquid and there is no transaction cost or tax.
7. The security market is efficient and purchases and sales by a single investors cannot affect the prices.

According to CAPM, systematic risk can be measured by (â) the beta factor. The â can be viewed as an index of the degree of the responsiveness of the security's returns with the market return. The beta coefficient is the relative measure of sensitivity of an asset's return to change in the return on the market portfolio. The beta coefficient (â) is calculated by relating the returns of a security with the returns for the market. Mathematically, the beta of security is the security's covariance with the market portfolio divided by the variance of the market portfolio and can be calculated as follows:

$$\beta = \frac{\text{Cov (S, M)}}{\sigma^2 \text{ M}} = \frac{\sigma_s \, \sigma_M \, \text{Cor}_{SM}}{\sigma^2 \text{ M}} = \frac{\sigma_S}{\sigma_M} \times \text{Cor}_{SM}$$

Where;

Cov(S,M) = Covariance between the return of security S, and the return on the market portfolio, M.

σ^2M = Variance of the return of market portfolio M

σ_S = Standard deviation of the Security, S

σ_M = Standard deviation of the market portfolio, M

Cor_{SM} = Correlation between the return of the security on the market portfolio

6.9 Summary

The identification and selection of an efficient portfolio is a complicated job. An investor must select a portfolio, which will best suit his requirements, out of all those available securities to him. According to Markowitz portfolio theory establishing the relationship between a portfolio's expected return and its level of risk as the criterion for selecting the optimum portfolio. The general rule for identifying attractive portfolio is that any portfolio offering a higher return for the same level of risk or a lower level of risk exposure for the same return, than another portfolio will be considered more attractive than the other portfolio.

The Capital Asset Pricing Model (CAPM) attempts to measure the risk of a security in the portfolio scene. The core idea of the CAPM is that only undiversifiable risk is relevant to the determination of expected return on any asset. In fact, the CAPM can be used to examine the risk and return of any type of capital asset such as individual security an investment project or a portfolio of assets/investment.

6.10 Key Words

1. *Feasible Set*: represents the set of all portfolios that can be formed and attainable by an investors out of several assets.
2. *Efficient Frontier*: is the set of portfolios of a given population of assets which offer the maximum possible expected return for a given level of risk.
3. *Construction of optimum portfolio*: refers to the allocation of funds among a variety of financial assets open for investment.

6.11 Questions

Short Questions

1. What is Portfolio?
2. What is Portfolio Section?
3. What is Portfolio Management?
4. What is Portfolio Analysis?

5. What is Efficient Portfolio?
6. What is Markowitz Model?
7. What is CAPM?
8. What is an Efficient Frontier?
9. How do you calculate risk of a portfolio?

Essay Questions

1. What is Markowitz optimation? Critically examine Markowitz model.
2. How do you analyse the dominance securities?
3. What is CAPM? Explain the theory with suitable examples.
4. Define and distinguish between portfolio analysis and security analysis.
5. What is portfolio diversification? How efficient diversification can be achieved?

6.12 Books for Further Reading

Elton, Edusin, J. and Gruber, Martin J. *Modern Portfolio Theory and Investment Analysis*, John Wiley & Sons, 1987.

Alexander, Gordon W.J. and Sharpe, William F. *Fundamental of Investments*, Prentice Hall, New Delhi.

V.A. Avadhani, *Investment and Securities Markets in India*, Himalaya Publishing House, Bombay.

7

PORTFOLIO INVESTMENT PROCESS

OBJECTIVES

The objectives of this unit are to:

- explain the portfolio investment process and its basic principles.
- discuss the portfolio types and their need.
- highlight the planning, implementation and monitoring, evaluation of portfolio suitability.
- describe the formula plans for investment.

7.1 Introduction

The portfolio once selected has to be continuously reviewed. Over a period of time and then revised depending on the objectives of the investor. The basic problem of portfolio management is to establish an investment goal or objectives and then decide how best to reach that or designed goal with the available securities. This has been stated as an attempt by the investor to obtain the maximum return with minimum risk. In order to do a proper job of portfolio management, the investor must be aware of the investment process. Therefore, the process of portfolio management involves a logical set of steps common to any decision. Such as plan, implement, and monitor. Based on this process selection of actual portfolio can be a complex, and opinion are divided on how best to select the portfolio investment process.

The following aspects of the investor are to be noted first in investment decisions.

1. The individual securities are important only to the extent that they affect the aggregate portfolio, and all decision should focus on the impact, the decision will have on the aggregate portfolio of an investor.
2. Larger expected portfolio returns come only with larger portfolio risk.
3. Diversification across the different securities will reduce the portfolio risk.
4. The portfolio strategy should be framed to the unique needs and characteristics of the portfolio's owner.

7.2 Types of Portfolios Depending upon the Investors Needs

Individuals and institution having different objectives and constraints own portfolios. The prospective investor's personal and financial information helps in deciding what kind of investment programme may be best suited to his needs. In the process of portfolio building, a suitable goal is to be established. The investor must determine how much risk is to be taken and then plan how to achieve these goals. The investor's goal may be growth or income or combination of both or as much income as moderately safety of principle with allow and so on, through many possibilities.

Types of Portfolios

Depending upon the investors needs and objectives of portfolios, the portfolio can be classified into the following three types.

1. High return with low risk portfolios.

2. High return with high-risk portfolios.
3. High return with comparatively high-risk portfolios.

One of the essential aspects of investment is to minimise risk. The investor wishes to accept risk consistent with gains, but not beyond, it would be imprudent to accept risk beyond what is necessary. Risk and return are correlated. It is proper to establish at trade off between risk and return, rather than under risk for a strong possibility of gains and loss. Hence, the investor should be conservative and act rationally when making investment decision within a general investment policy such as buy equity shares only, investors may decide to buy growth shares only. They may further concentrate on speculative growth shares rather than quality growth shares.

All investors prefer those securities, which have a high return but at the same time the risk attached to it is low. At the time of combining the securities and constructing a portfolio of different combination of securities an investor is faced with problems of risk and return.

Portfolio objectives will largely determine the investment strategy. The following aspects may achieve the different objectives:

1. Balancing fixed interest securities against equities.
2. Balancing high dividend payment companies against high earnings growth companies as required.
3. Finding the income or growth portfolio as required.
4. Balancing transaction costs against capital gains from rapid switching.
5. Balancing income tax payable against capital gains tax.
6. Retaining some liquidity to seize upon bargains.

7.3 Steps to Portfolio Investment Process

The portfolio investment process and management involves the following logical set of steps:

1. Planning
2. Implementation
3. Monitoring
4. Evaluation.

1. Planning

Planning is the most important element of proper portfolio investment. Planning refers identification of investor's objectives, constraints and preferences, which will help formulate the investment policy. The study of investors condition, market condition, investment or speculative polices, statement of investment policy and strategic asset, allocation are the aspects of planning stage.

3. Implementation

The next stage, namely, implementation and execution of the investment process. Implementation and execution is the most critical process in the portfolio management. Implementation stage begins by periodically adjusting the asset mix to the desired mix called for in the strategic asset allocation. Tactical asset allocation and security selection decisions are made. Many portfolio owners engage in speculative transaction in the belief that such transactions will generate excess risk adjusted returns. Such speculative transactions are usually classified as "Timing" or "Selection" decisions. Timing decisions over or under weight various asset classes, industries or economic sectors from the strategic asset allocation. Such timing decisions have come to be known as tactical asset allocation decisions. Whereas, the selection decisions deal with securities within a given asset class, industry group or economic sector and attempt to determine which securities should be over (or) under-weighted.

4. Monitoring

Portfolio monitoring is a continuous on-going assessment of the current portfolio to the goals, changes in investor's preferences, capital market conditions and expectations. The monitoring requires a periodic meeting with investors to know the changes in the conditions, continuous review of the investment policy relative to investor's preferences. The following three aspects will be involved in the portfolio monitoring.

1. Firstly, the actual portfolio held should be examined to ascertain that it is in compliance with the statement of investment policy and to determine whether any passive re-balancing of the asset mix is required.
2. Secondly, investment performance should be reviewed. This should consist of review of returns on the aggregate portfolio, each asset class and investment manager, and the returns from any speculative strategies employed.
3. Finally, adjustments to the statement of investment policies and investment managers should be made if necessary.

5. *Evaluation*

The portfolio performance is evaluated by comparing the yield of managed portfolios with the market index or with a random portfolio. When two portfolios are compared, managed and unmanaged the portfolio with the higher holding period yield will be considered the best portfolio. Through this method it can be found out if the returns on managed portfolios have performed better than any unmanaged portfolios. But in comparing these portfolios the cost of commission and risk has to be compared also. There are several models for evaluating the performance of portfolio.

7.4 Formula Plans for Investment

The formula plans give the basic rules and regulations for purchasing and selling of investments. These plans are predetermined with distinctive objective and rigidity of rates.

The investors use formula plans to help them in making decisions for the future by exploiting the fluctuations in prices. It helps the investors to assess the total amount that they should spend on purchases. One of the aspects of these formula plans is to have a set of rigid and ground rules, which are devoid of any emotions, or feelings of the person who is making purchases. These plans are action-oriented and eliminate the feelings of a person who wishes to make in the thinking of security purchase for the construction of a portfolio so that the investor does not make loss. The investor must note that these formula plans do not help in the selection of securities. The selection of securities will have to be done by some other technique.

Rules for Formula Plans

1. The formula plans are useful for making a decision on the timing of investments.
2. The formula plans are strict, rigid and straightforward but, they are not flexible.
3. The formula plans cannot be used or found useful for short period of time.
4. The formula plans do not eliminate the need for making forecast.
5. The formula plans work according to methodology, which is related for the working of each plan.

Types of Formula Plans

The investor uses formula plans to help him in making decisions for the future by exploiting the fluctuations in prices. In this purpose the formula plans are to be identified into the following three types:

(i) The constant rupee value plan

(ii) The constant ratio plan

(iii) The variable ratio plan

(i) The Constant Rupee Value Plan

The constant rupee value plan specifies that the rupee value of the stock portion of the portfolio will remain constant. This formula plan indicates to the investor that whenever the stock value rises his shares should be sold to maintain a constant portfolio. According to this formula the investor should buy shares when prices fall to maintain a constant portfolio. This formula plan also indicates to the investors how to place the action point, (i.e.) the period of time when action should be taken. If the action points are too close together then there will be no profits as the transfer will be expensive and the transaction cost will be high. The main limitation of the constant rupee value plan is that it requires some initial forecasting. However, it does not require forecasting the extent to which upward fluctuations may reach.

(ii) Constant Ratio Plan

Constant ratio plan is slightly different from the constant rupee value plan. This plan is a method of identifying the ratio of the value in the aggressive portfolio to the value of the conservative portfolio. The constant ratio plan holder can adjust portfolio balance either at fixed intervals or when the portfolio moves away from the desired ratio by a fixed percentage. Under this plan the constant ratio can be determined by the following formula:

$$K = \frac{\text{Market value of common stock}}{\text{Market value of total portfolio}}$$

(iii) Variable Ratio Plan

The variable ratio plan moves and works with indicators. These indicators are the market index or the economic activity index and the moving averages determined of the market index. Instead of maintaining a constant rupee amount in stocks or a constant ratio of stocks to bonds, the variable ratio plan uses steadily lowers the aggressive portion of the total portfolio as stock prices rise, and steadily increases the aggressive portion as stock prices fall, by changing the proportions of defensive aggressive holdings, the investor is in effect buying stock more aggressively as stock prices fall and selling stock more aggressively as stock prices rise.

7.5 Summary

The process of portfolio management involves a logical set of steps common to any decision, such as planning implementation and monitoring. Portfolios are owned by individuals and institutions having different objectives and constraints. The prospective investor's personal and financial information helps in deciding what kind of investment programme may be best suited to his needs. All investors prefer these securities which have a high return but at the same time the risk attached to it is low. At the time of combining the securities and constructing a portfolio of different combinations of securities on investor is faced with same question of risk and return.

Formula plans give the basic rules and regulations for purchasing and selling of investments. These help the investor to assess the total amount that he should spend on purchase. One of the aspects of these formula plans is to have a set of rigid and ground rules, which are devoid of any emotions, or feelings of the person who is making purchases. The three main formula plans for investors who have already an accumulated fund are the constant rupee value plan, the constant ratio plan, and the variable ratio plan. These plans have a method of building two portfolios; the conservative portfolio and the aggressive portfolio.

7.6 Key Words

Constant rupee value plan — It is the simplest form of formula plans and every investor can work according to this plan without making complicated calculations.

Constant ratio plan	The plan is a method of identifying the ratio of the value in the aggressive portfolio to the value of the conservative portfolio.
Variable ratio plan	The methodology of the formula plan should have a pre-determined set of rules and consist of different proportions of stock prices. Under this plan the ratio of value of aggressive portfolio, the value of conservative portfolio, decreases when the aggressive portfolio rises in value.

7.8 Questions

1. Explain the types portfolios depending upon the investors needs.
2. Discuss the various steps involved in portfolio investment process.
3. What are formula plans? How do they help in portfolio revision?

7.9 Books for Further Reading

1. Fischer and Jordon, *Security Analysis and Portfolio Management*, Prentice Hall, Engle wood Cliffs, New Jersey, USA, 1983.
2. Clark Francis, *Management of Investments*, McGraw International student edition, New York, 1983.
3. William I. Shape, *Portfolio Theory and Capital Markets*, McGraw Hill USA, 1970.

8

MEASUREMENT OF PORTFOLIO PERFORMANCE

OBJECTIVES

The Objectives of this lesson are to:

- distinguish between performance measurement and performance evaluation.
- discuss the various concepts and methods of computing portfolio return.
- highlight the measures of risk adjusted return methods viz., Sharpe's model and Treynor's model.

8.1 Introduction

Performance measurement is an accounting function, which attempts to compare the performance at the end of period with that at the beginning of the period. Whereas, the portfolio performance is generally evaluated over a time interval of at least four years, with returns for a number of sub-periods within the interval-like monthly or quarterly, so that there is a fairly adequate numbers of observations for statistical evaluation. The calculation of portfolio return is fairly simple when there are no deposits or withdrawals of money from a portfolio during a time period. In this case, the market value of the portfolio in the beginning and at the end of the periods is determined by computing the portfolio return. The performance evaluation addresses the issues of whether:

- the past performance was superior or inferior?
- such performance was due to skill or luck?
- future performance will be similar or not?

Performance measurement becomes difficult when a client adds or withdraws money from the portfolio. The percent change in the market value of the portfolio computed may not be an accurate measurement of portfolio's return. In the event of a deposit or a withdrawal occurring just after the commencement of the period, the return on the portfolio should be calculated by adjusting the beginning market value of portfolio. In the case of deposits, the beginning value would be increased by the deposit amount and in the case of withdrawal, the beginning value would be decreased by the amount.

8.2 Measures of Return Using Sharpe's and Treynor's Model

The portfolio performance can be measured under different models. The choice of model or method will depend on the performance evaluation objectives Broadly these models are as follows:

1. Dollar-Weighted Rate of Return Model.
2. Time-Weighted Return Model.
3. Risk Adjusted Return Model.

If the performance of the fund is being evaluated, dollar-weighted return model would be appropriate as it provides the return from the perspective of the client. If the investment manager's decisions were being evaluated, the time-weighted return would be appropriate, as it would exclude the effect of the clients' cash flow decisions. Whereas, the risk adjusted return model gives an idea of whether the return earned is commensurate with the risk faced. The performance of a fund should be assessed in terms of return per unit of risk. The funds, which provide the highest return per unit of risk would be considered the best performer.

Sharpe's model and Treynor's models are well known measures of risk adjusted returns of the portfolio.

Sharpe's Performance Model

The Sharpe's performance measure takes into account measurement of the risk premium for performance of the portfolios. This model adjusts the performance for risk. Under this model portfolio performance can be measured by the following formula:

$$S_t = \frac{r_p - r_f}{\sigma p}$$

Where;

S_t = Sharpe's index of desirability.

r_p = Average return of portfolio.

r_f = Risk free rate of return.

σ = Standard deviation of risk of the returns of portfolio.

Sharpe's model involves the procedure of first subtracting from each portfolio's net average return [r_p] on estimate of the risk-free rate [r_f] over the evaluation period. This difference can be viewed as a risk premium or rewards for investing in assets with more than zero risk. Then each portfolio's risk premium is divided by its standard deviation of annual returns, [ó], a measure of the portfolio's total risk or variability estimated over the evaluation period. The resulting figure [S_t] is the ratio of reward per unit of variability. Thus, the Sharpe's index of desirability, known as the reward to variability ratio, and it can be used for comparing portfolios in different risk classes. It can be presented graphically as follows:

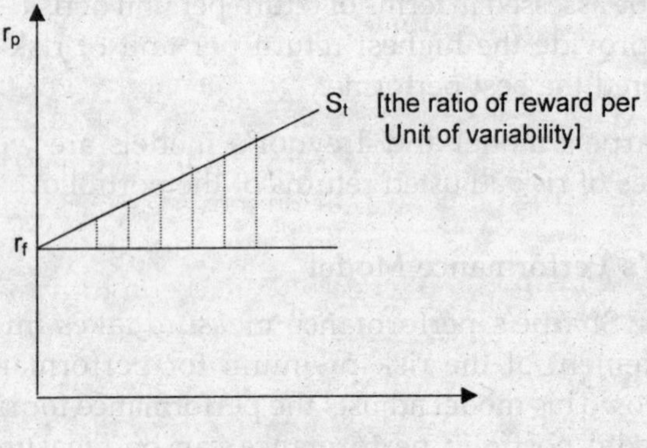

Performance Measurement by Sharpe's index [S_t]

According to the Sgharpe's index graphic presentation, it can be found that the changer S_t will present better performance of the portfolio.

Treynor's Portfolio Performance Model

Treynor's model is another risk-adjusted model for measuring the performance of portfolio. Treynor's model is based on the concept of the characteristic straight line. It gives both the linear and curvilinear relationship. The graphical description of Treynor's performance measure is as follows:

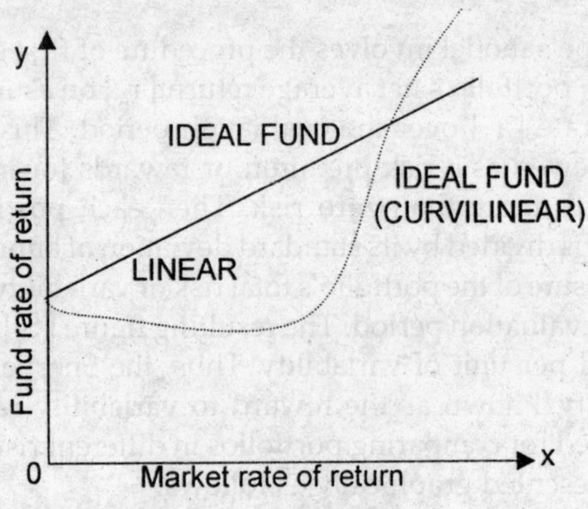

Treynor's Performance Model

According to graphical presentation the inter-section at 45° angle represents that return which is equivalent to the return on the market portfolio. The ideal fund is shown to the left of 45° line. This is also above the imaginary 45° line. The return on this line is higher than that which is earned on the market portfolio. Thus, the portfolio shows a negative return under this model is positive but, if the market return is positive the return under the model of the characteristic line is still higher.

The portfolio performance can be measured by Treynors model with the help of the following formula

$$T_n = \frac{r_p - r_f}{\beta p}$$

Where;

T_n = Treynor's index of desirability

r_p = Average return of portfolio

r_f = Risk free rate of return

β_p = Beta coefficient of portfolio

The Treynor's model measures the systematic risk premium of the portfolio and takes into consideration difference on the return of a portfolio and the risk rate.

8.3 Sharpe's Vs Treynor's Measures

Sharpe's and Treynor's measures provide a way of ranking the relative performance of various portfolios on a risk-adjusted basis. For investors whose portfolio is a predominant representation in a particular asset class, the total variability of return as measured by standard deviation is the: relevant risk measures. The ranking on both these measures will be identical when both the funds are well diversified. A poorly diversified fund will rank lower according to the Sharpe's measure than the Treynor's model. The less diversified fund will show greater risk and which can be measured by using standard deviation.

The Sharpe measure uses the standard deviation [ó] of returns as the measure of risk, while Treynor's measure employs beta [â]. Therefore, the two measures provide complementary but different information and both measures should be derived. As pointed out by Sharpe, if one is dealing with a well-diversified group of portfolios, such as mutual funds, the two measures will provide very similar rankings. Because Sharpe felt the variability due to unsystematic risk was probably transitory, he felt that the Treynor's measure might be a better measure for predicting future performance, and his results generally confirmed this expectation.

8.4 Summary

In this unit we have distinguished between performance measured and performance evaluation. We have also discussed various concepts and methods of computing portfolio return. Risk adjusted rate of return is one of such methods. Sharpe's and Treynor's models are well known measures of risk adjusted return method. Both these measures provide a way of ranking the relative performance of various portfolios on a risk-adjusted basis. The ranking on both these measures will be identical when both the funds are well diversified. The Sharpe's measure uses the standard deviation of returns as the measure of risk, while the Treynor's measure employs beta. The two measures would give identical rankings because the total variance of the portfolio would be a systematic variance.

8.5 Key Words

Dollar-weighted Rate of Return

The internal rate of return that equates the initial contribution and the cash flows that occur during the period with the ending value of the fund is the Dollar Weighted Rate of Return.

Time Weighted Return

The time-weighted rate of return is the weighted average

of the internal rates of return for the sub-periods between the cash flows and it is weighted by the length of the sub-periods.

Risk Adjusted Return

Risk-adjusted return gives an idea of whether the return earned is commensurate with risk incurred. Under this method the performance of a fund should be assessed in terms of return per unit of risk.

8.6 Questions

1. Write a note on:
   (a) Sharpe's Performance Measure
   (b) Treynor's Performance Measure
2. What is the essential difference between the Sharope's and Treynor's Model of Portfolio Performance?

8.7 Books for Further Readings

1. Fischer and Jordan, *Security Analysis and Portfolio Management*, Prentice Hall, 1983.
2. Fredrick Amling, *Investments – An Introduction to Analysis and Management*, USA, 1984.
3. William F. Sharpe & Gordon, J. Alexander, *Investments*, Prentice Hall of India, New Delhi, 1994.

9
MUTUAL FUNDS

OBJECTIVES

The objectives of the lesson are to:

- explain, the concept of mutual funds and their objectives
- describe the various types of mutual funds
- study the applications of security analysis to the mutual fund industry
- observe the fund management process of mutual funds
- explore the recent developments in mutual funds in India

9.1 Introduction

Mutual funds are trusts of public who will invest in the financial instruments for the mutual benefits of its members. The mutual funds will pool the accumulated savings from public and invest them in a diversified portfolio of financial assets. The portfolio will be constructed with a view to reduce risks and maximise return to their members. The members will enjoy the return on a pro-rata basis. They utilise collectively the benefits of experitized investment by specialists of the trust. Therefore, the services of such specialist could not possible to avail by the individual investors. Hence, the mutual fund is based on a concept of mutual help of the subscribers for portfolio investment. The mutual funds are set up under the Indian Trust Act. These funds cater mainly to individual investors and small investors. The business of the mutual funds attracted the interest of the financial community and is growing at a rapid pace in India.

9.2 Concept of Mutual Funds

The concept of mutual fund was conceived to pool the resources of small investors and deploy the same in the capital market to help industrialisation through participation in equity and other debt instruments. The mutual funds offer the investors the advantage of diversified portfolio and professional management at low cost. Informed investment, safety of funds, dispersal of risks and reasonably satisfactory yield are the essential features of the mutual funds.

Definition

Various authors have defined mutual fund in different ways. According to Pierce James "Mutual fund is a non-depository, non-banking financial intermediary which acts as important vehicle for bringing wealth holders and deficit units together indirectly".

Weston J. Fred and Brigham defined mutual fund as "A corporation which accepts money from investors and uses the same to key stocks, long-term bonds, short-term debt instruments issued by business or government. These corporations pool funds and thus reduce risk by diversification.

9.3 Objectives of Mutual Funds

The objectives of the mutual funds are presented below:

1. To provide an opportunity to the small investors for entering into the capital and money markets.
2. To act as a catalyst to divert the small savings towards stock market activities.

3. To mobilise savings of Non-resident savers.
4. To enable the investors to share the benefits of the capital market.
5. To achieve investment variety and spread in different industries.
6. To receive the investors from investment analysis, paperwork and monitoring.
7. To provide tax benefits on the invested amounts/ returns or dividends/ capital gains.

9.4 History of Mutual Funds

The mutual fund system has started thousands of years ago. In the past Egyptians and phoneticians had followed a system of risk sharing. They began to sold shares in vessels and caravans in order to spread the risk. After a long time the King William I of Netherlands was formed an investment trust in 1822 for the benefits of risk sharing. The present system of mutual fund had taken birth in USA in 1930. The first mutual fund in India was started by the Unit Trust of India in 1964. It was established under the Unit Trust of India Act, 1963. It is the only mutual fund operating from 1964. It is the public sectors mutual fund and set up UTI bank in 1987. The Banking Regulation Act was amended in 1983 to permit the banks to carry non-banking business activities such as mutual funds leasing etc. Therefore, the public sector banks such as the SBI, Canara Bank, Punjab National Bank have set up their own mutual funds. The other two financial institutions LIC, and GIC have also set up their mutual funds in 1989 and 1990 respectively. The mutual funds of LIC and GIC were regulated by the Ministry of Finance.

9.5 Regulation of Mutual Funds

In 1992 the government permitted for setting up of mutual funds in the private and public sector. Recently the public sector development banks like IDBI and ICICI have been permitted to set up mutual funds. The government also permitted the foreign mutual funds to commence the business operations in India. All the mutual funds in India will be regulated by RBI, Ministry of Finance and the SEBI. SEBI is the most powerful organisation to control, regulate monitor the mutual fund sector in India. The RBI is the regulatory authority in case of mutual funds established by the banks. At present mutual funds are governed by the following guidelines.

(a) RBI guidelines

(b) SEBI guidelines

9.6 Classification of Mutual Funds

Mutual funds are classified into two kinds:

(a) Open ended mutual funds

(b) Close ended mutual funds

9.7 Open-ended Mutual Funds

In the open ended mutual fund scheme the units are available for sale throughout the year. There is no ceiling on the units for the sale. The units, which are allotted to the investors, are called as unit holders. The fund can redeem the outstanding units at anytime. There is no opening and closing time for these schemes. The open-ended scheme provides liquidity to the unit holders. Unit holders can sale his units whenever he wants. The purchase and sale price of the units is fixed by the mutual fund on the basis of "Net Asset value" of the units. Therefore the NAV is the most important factor in the mutual fund sector. The NAV will be calculated by the fund and it will be published at least once in a week. The number of units of open-ended fund varies from day to day basis. Open-ended funds are managed, issued and operated by the fund managers as per the regulations of the SEBI. The NAV of the open-ended fund change for everyday. The open-ended funds are quite popular among the investors. These schemes will assure the investors dividends, capital appreciation, safety and liquidity. The mutual funds are legally bound to repurchase the units. The value of the units are influenced by the NAV. The NAV of the unit can be calculated by the following formula.

$$\text{NAV} = \frac{\text{Total market value of the assets in the portfolio- Liabilities}}{\text{Number of fund units (shares) outstanding}}$$

OR

$$\text{NAV} = \frac{\text{Market value of the fund's assets}}{\text{The number of outstanding unit of the fund}}$$

The formula used to calculate the sale and repurchase prices of units are as follows:

$$\text{Sale price} = \frac{(\text{Market value of assets} - \text{liabilities}) + (\text{operating expenses})^2}{\text{Number of units outstanding}}$$

$$\text{Repurchase price} = \frac{\begin{array}{c}(\text{Market value of assets} - \text{liabilities (excluding contingent} \\ \text{Liabilities, initial share capital, reserves and unit capital)} \\ - \text{ Brokerage commission}\end{array}}{\text{Number of units issued or outstanding}}$$

9.8 Close Ended Mutual Funds

The close-ended funds are fixed in size as regards the corpus of the fund and the number of shares. No fresh units are created in these funds after the origin of the scheme expires. The close ended fund scheme will sell the units at a fixed time. The units are offered to public when the issue is open for subscription. It has fixed time duration for the operation of the scheme. They do not sell any additional units after the sale of a fixed number of units at the initial stage. The scheme corpus fund remains fixed till their redemption. The schemes have a lock in period of 3 to 5 years. They may offer a guaranteed dividend. The units of the close-ended are not redeemed by mutual funds before the termination of the period of the scheme. The units will be listed on the stock market and can be traded the investors. This scheme offers liquidity and transparency to the investors.

9.9 Types of Mutual funds

Depending on the objectives, the funds can be classified into the following categories:

(i) Money market mutual funds (MMMF)

(ii) Growth oriented funds

(iii) Income funds

(iv) Balanced funds

(v) Specialised funds

(vi) Offshore funds

(vii) Tax free funds

(viii) Index funds

(ix) Customers group funds

(x) Sector funds

i) Money Market Mutual Funds (MMMF)

The RBI permitted the money market mutual fund scheme in April 1992. It provides an additional avenue to the individual investors. The RBI relaxed some conditions in order to attract more investors. A series of relaxations were announced at the beginning. The maximum limit of the fund to be raised was at Rs. 50 crores but at later this restriction was removed. Now the private sector mutual funds are allowed to set up these funds. The banks are allowed to set up these funds. The schemes are offered to individual investors and corporate. Now, the scheme was liberalised and the lock in period was brought down to 15 days. The scheme provides better liquidity and ready market to the investors. The investment should be confined to call money, certificate of deposits, commercial papers, commercial bills, treasury bills, and dated government securities. The MMMF schemes offer high liquidity and better returns than bank deposits. The return on the money market mutual funds will be higher at 8 to 12%. The return may be in the form of bonus or capital appreciation. The low liquidity and high returns are available from commercial bills Company Deposit Schemes 9CDS) and Commercial paper Schemes (CPS). The other financial instruments have high liquidity but low returns. The popularity of these funds with the common investors is yet to gain. SEBI is the regulatory authority to grant the permission to operate the MMMF. The sponsor of MMF should be a registered company or scheduled bank or all India level financial institution with good track record. Sponsoring company should have at least 40% of equity in the paid up equity of the MMMF.

ii) Growth-Oriented Funds

Mutual funds offer growth-oriented schemes to the investors. These schemes are offered to meet the investors need to make money for long term purpose. These funds are aimed at achieving capital appreciation. These funds do not offer fixed regular returns but provide substantial capital appreciation in the long run. The pattern of investment is general oriented towards share of high growth companies. The growth scheme is more useful to the long-term objectives of the investors. These schemes are offered to all kinds of investors. The amount of money collected by these schemes will be invested in the growth-oriented securities. Generally 80% of the collected amount will be deployed in their segment. These schemes are useful to the investors to meet the purpose of their children's marriage or education or social customs. This scheme does not provide liquidity.

The growth funds invest primarily in equities and speculative investments. The following are the examples of growth schemes.

(1) Primary equity fund (UTI)

(2) Grand master (UTI)

(3) Master gain (UTI)

(4) UGS-5000 (UTI)

(5) Master Share (UTI)

(6) Magnum Triple Plus Scheme (SBI MF)

(7) Can stock, can growth can share (Can Bank MF)

(8) Equity growth fund (PNB MF)

(9) Growth plus (GIC MF)

(10) Morgan Stanley growth fund (Kothari MF)

iii) Income Funds

Income funds are targeted towards high current income and create low risk to the investors. It offers regular income to the investors. These funds offer a return much higher than the bank deposits but with less capital appreciation. The emphasis being on regular returns, the pattern of investment is also oriented towards fixed income yielding securities such as convertible debentures of consistently good dividend companies. They will pay the funds return on the monthly basis. The pensioners, rural income groups and urban average groups attract it. These kinds of people depend on the income to meet their regular expenditure. The following are the examples of income oriented funds.

(1) U.S. 64(UTI)

(2) Magnum Monthly Income Plan (SBI MF)

(3) Dhana Shree (LIC MF)

(4) GIC Safe (GIC MF)

iv) Balanced Funds

Balanced funds will combine the income and growth. These offer a blend of immediate average returns and reasonable capital appreciation in the long run. The investment portfolio of these funds is evenly distributed among fixed income bearing corporate securities and common stock with growth potential. Funds investment portfolio consists of securities, which facilitates to generate income as well as capital appreciation. The balanced fund is also known as "Income cum growth funds". The aim of the fund is to provide a regular income and

(h) The MFs are not allowed to invest more than 15% of its funds in the shares and debentures of any specific industry.

(i) The MFs are not allowed to involve in short selling or carry forward transactions or bad finances.

(j) The MFs should take physical delivery of shares for purchases and deliver the scrips on sale of shares.

(k) Transfers from one scheme to another scheme are allowed subject to the same conditions.

9.12 Recent Developments in Mutual Funds

One of the important features of the mutual fund is that most of them are already in leasing and hire purchase business. All the mutual funds do not get tax benefits like UTI, hence they are entering into leasing business as a tax shield. Most of these mutual funds are investing in the equities of fast growing companies. This ambition for growth may prove trouble to some funds. The mutual funds have been getting the expert services from banking, finance and academic fields with a view to introduce the professionalism. Another important development in this area is the organisation of mutual funds by the reputed industrial houses like, Tata's, Birla's, Reliance etc. collaboration of foreign banks to tap non-resident investments. These funds would be utilised for investment in shares of Indian companies, for setting new projects involving high technology.

Another important set up of the public sector mutual funds is the splitting of the UTI into two organisation such UTI-I and UTI-II. The UTI-I will be the public sector, where as UTI-II will be slowly privatised. On account of this development the private sectors, mutual funds will gain prominence in the mutual fund business.

The future prospects of mutual funds are considerably very bright in view of expanding investors support and initiation of the novel proposals by the government of India and mutual funds. The recent developments in the mutual funds business are listed below:

(i) Launching of several new varieties of schemes offering triple benefits of income, liquidity and growth.

(ii) Introduction of tax benefit schemes to attract the taxpayers to reduce the tax liability under section 88 of Indian Income Tax Act-1961.

(iii) The budget for 1992-93 has given tax exemption for the mutual fund income under income tax act. This will encourage the setting up of new mutual funds in India both in joint and private sectors.

(iv) The government has been encouraging the private sector to set up mutual funds as per the guidelines of SEBI.

9.13 Summary

The mutual fund is based on the concept of mutual help of the subscribers for portfolio investment. The mutual funds are governed by rules of RBI and SEBI. Mutual funds are classified into two kinds viz., open ended and close-ended funds. The units of open-ended funds are available for sale on a continuous basis to the investors. Close-ended funds are available only on a particular period of time. The various types of mutual funds are available in India are MMMF, Growth funds, income fund, balanced fund, specialised fund, offshore fund, tax free fund, index fund, area fund, customers group fund, and sector funds. The mutual funds provide many advantages to the investors. Mutual funds are allowed to invest only in transferable securities either in the money market or capital market. UTI is the oldest mutual fund in India. It comes into operation from 1964. It extends financial assistance to the corporate sector by way of term loans and involved underwriting the public issues. It also grants long-term loans and involved in the hire purchasing, leasing, housing finances etc.

9.14 Key Words

Open ended scheme : The units are available for sale

		throughout the year for the investors.
Close ended Scheme	:	The units are offered to the public for a fixed period.
NAV	:	Net Asset value is the barometer of the fund. It reveals the performance of the fund.
MMMF	:	Money Market Mutual fund is a short-term fund. It can be opened with the permission of the SEBI and RBI.
Off-shore fund	:	This kind of schemes is introduced to Attract the foreign capital.
Index funds	:	Index funds are associated with the stock market index. The value of index fund depends upon the stock market index.

9.15 Questions

1. What is Mutual fund? What are the advantages to the investors?
2. Explain various types of mutual fund schemes.
3. Discuss the investment restrictions imposed by the SEBI on mutual funds.
4. Discuss the various schemes issued in India by the mutual funds?
5. What is Net Asset value? How is it calculated? What is its usefulness?

9.16 Suggested Readings

1. G.S. Batra & R.C. Dangwal, *Financial services – New Innovations*, Deep and Deep Publications, New Delhi.

2. *Mutual Funds: Business Week,* June 11, 1990.

3. Lucile Tomlinson (ed) 1971, *How to Start, Operate and Manage Mutual Funds,* Presidents Pub. House, New York.

4. Gangadhar, V, The Changing Pattern of Mutual Funds in India, *The Management Accountant*, December 1992.

10
FINANCIAL DERIVATIVES

OBJECTIVES

The objectives of this lesson are to:

explain the concept of derivatives and their objectives.

discuss the risks of derivatives management

study the recent trends in the derivatives market.

explain the components of derivatives.

10.1 Introduction

The Indian economy has been experiencing a dynamic change since 1991 due to introduction of liberalisation, privatisation and globalisation policies. The economic reforms were introduced to correct various distortions and disorientation. The new economic policy aimed at correcting the imbalances and creating a more competitive environment to improve productivity and efficiency. In the new economic environment, series of structural changes were undertaken in financial sector reforms to achieve the objectives. The financial sector reforms have encompassed reform programmes in banking sector, capital market and removal of controls over capital issues and issues pricing etc. The capital market reforms include the setting up of Securities and Exchange Board of India and its guidelines for mutual funds, permitting the selected companies to raise capital from abroad with tax benefits, allowing foreign investors to invest in India capital market. The financial sector reforms are expected to give a boost to the economy by allocating funds for productive investment and for capital formation. The operational investment in the financial system is expected to facilitate and expedite the process of the market information.

The Indian stock market, inspite of being insulated from the international markets is characterised by high price volatility. Speculation extends to non-specified shares also and speculative dealings are supposed to be settled on a cash basis. In the case of new issues, before they are listed in the exchange, investors suffer heavy losses due to the "area market operations". However, speculation is unavoidable, as it is a driving force, which builds up activity and ensures sustained interest of investors. The presence of speculators is useful for maintaining market continuity. The central government seeks to control any excessive speculation, which leads haphazard price movements unrelated to fundamentals of securities.

In the present state of the economy, there is an imperative need for the corporate clients to protect their operating profits by shifting some of the uncontrollable financial risks to those who are able to bear and manage them. Thus the risk of management becomes a must for survival, since there is a high volubility in the present financial market.

In this context derivatives occupy an important place as a risk reducing machinery. Derivatives are useful to reduce the risks. In this context the financial service companies can play a dominant role in dealing with such risks. They can ensure that the risks are hedged by using various derivative components such as future, options and swaps etc. Thus the derivatives enable the clients to transfer their financial risks to financial service companies. This will protect the investors from the unforeseen risks and helps them to get their due operating profits. To hedge the various risks that one faces in financial market to day, derivatives are absolute necessary.

10.2 Concept of Derivatives

Derivatives derive their value from an underlying asset. For instance, equity share itself is a derivative. Since it derives its value from the firm's underlying assets. If a person takes an insurance policy against his property covering all risks is also a derivative instrument on the property. The derivatives are based on all those major financial instruments, which are explicitly traded like equities, debt investment, forex instruments and commodity based on contracts. The derivatives originate in mathematics and refer to a variable, which has been derived from another financial product or commodity. The derivatives do not have independent existence without under lying product and market. Derivatives are contracts, which are written between two parties for easily marketable assets. Derivatives are also known as deferred delivery or deferred payment instruments. Derivatives can be defined as a "financial product, which has been derived from another financial product or commodity".

D.G. Gardener defined the derivatives as "a financial product which has been derived from market for another product "Derivatives are off balance sheet instruments, a fact that is said to obscure the leverage and financial might they give to the party. Derivatives have little usefulness in mobilising fresh capital by the companies. The exchange-traded derivatives are quite liquid and have low transactions cost. There is a lot of demand in India for derivatives trading. The values of derivatives are those of their underlying assets are closely related. Bombay Stock Exchange and National Stock Exchange have introduced the financial derivatives in India. Derivatives would only enhance further, the speculative potential of the already highly speculative Indian stock market.

10.3 Objectives of Derivatives :

The main objectives of derivatives are as follows:

1. Hedging
2. Speculation

3. Price discovery
4. Allocation of resources
5. Transactional efficiency

1. *Hedging*

Hedging seeks to protect the investors against price changes in a commodity or derivatives in which they are interested. The speculators trade on future with an objective of profit from price changes. Hedging is the process of shifting unwanted price risks to others. In the derivatives market the hedging helps the investors to passion the price risk inherent in the business to traders, who are willing to take risk. In this process the commercial uses of the markets can hedge their price risks and by doing so, they will minimise the art of doing the business. This provides a way for an efficient market system and lowers costs to the investors.

2. *Speculation*

Earning extra-ordinary profits from the changes in the prices of financial assets is the objective of the speculators. Speculators forecast the prices well in advance and buy the financial assets now itself and store it for the period up to his expected prices comes, sell the holding and gains the profit. The speculator will buy the future contracts that permit them to take delivery of the asset after price rises and he earns profits. If the price fall than the purchase price will lose the profit. To avoid such type of heavy losses by the speculators, they will enter in to the trading of financial derivative components such as futures, options and minimise the expected loss.

3. *Price discovery*

The price discovery represents the ability to achieve and disseminate price information. Without price information the investors, consumers and produces can not make informed decisions. They are then face problems of diverting the capital for efficient use. Derivatives are exceptionally well suited for the role of providing price information. They are the tools that assist every one in the market to determine the value. The wider the use of derivatives, the wider the distribution of price information.

4. ***Allocation of resources***

Equilibrium or accurate prices allows both the consumers and producers to make better decisions with regard to which commodities to consume, which to produce, how to produce them and the quantity to produce and consume in the present and future, thus the more accurate prices result in superior allocation of resources.

5. ***Transactional efficiency***

Transactional efficiency is the product of liquidity. Inadequate liquidity results in high transaction costs. This impedes the investments and determines the accumulation of capital. Derivatives facilitate the opposite result. They significantly increase the market liquidity. As a result the transactional costs are reduced, the efficiency in doing business is increased, the cost of raising capital is lowered and the amount of capital available for productive investment is expanded.

10.4 Players in the Derivatives

There are 3 major players in the derivatives trading.

(a) Hedgers

(b) Speculators

(c) Arbitrageurs

(a) Hedgers

The party, which manages the risk, is known as hedger. Hedger seeks to protect themselves against price changes in a commodity in which they have an interest.

(b) Speculators

Speculators are the major players in the market, without whom the market probably would never exist.

(c) Arbitrageurs

These are specialised in making purchases and sales in different markets at the same time and profits by the difference in prices between the two centres.

A diagram shows derivatives market players.

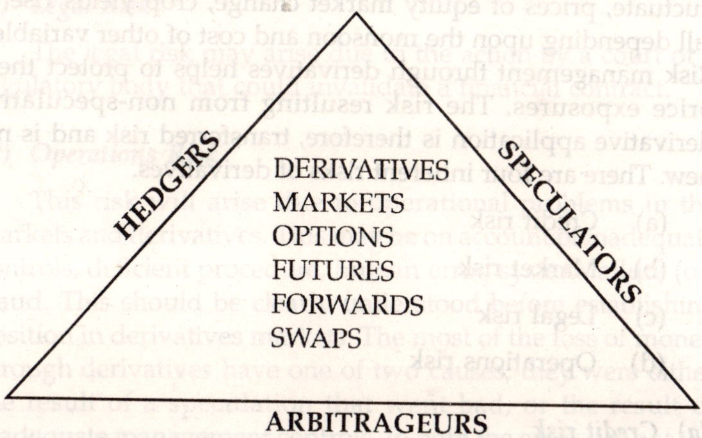

10.5 Advantages of Derivatives :

The following are the advantages of derivatives.

1. These increase the volume of transaction.
2. Facilitates lower transaction cost.
3. Increase hedging for investors in cash market.
4. Provide liquidity for investors.
5. Channels small savings towards the market.
6. Help to fasten execution of transactions
7. Enhance the price discovery process

to problems when the demand for the economy reach beyond the capacity of the group and the group has to expand. The policies of liberalisation, privatisation and globlisation since 1991 have generated price fluctuations and enhanced volatility in the markets. This has led to a natural need for the market instruments, which help in risk management.

In India all attempts are being made to introduce derivative instruments in the capital market. The Bombay Stock Exchange and the National Stock Exchange have introduced index-based futures. A stiff net worth criteria of Rs.7.00 to Rs.10.00 crores cover is proposed for members who which to enroll for such trading.

In the forex market there are various derivatives put to operation on the recommendation of the high level committee appointed by the RBI under the chairmanship of Mr.O.P.Sodhani, the RBI has introduced the derivatives in forex markets also.

However, there is need for effective control and implementation of derivatives contracts. The advantage of derivatives can be derived only when there is a transparency with the honest dealings. The players in the derivatives must have a sound financial position for dealing in the derivative transactions. The success of a derivatives market depends on determination of proper capital adequacy norms training of financial intermediaries and provision of well-established indices.

The Reserve Bank of India has liberalised the policy on derivatives in October, 1996. According to the guide lines issued by the RBI the commercial can offer to hedge instruments to the corporate.

These guidelines are presented below:

1. Authorised dealers in the forex market can offer currency Swaps, Cross Currency Swaps, Cross Currency Options and forward rate agreement.

2. The financial derivatives can be offered to book the overseas transactions.

3. Options will be allowed to sell to the customers by authorised dealers only.
4. The authorised dealers are required to get the final approval from the RBI.
5. Corporate bodies have to maintain and furnish the reports to RBI with in a week.

10.8 Summary of the Lesson

The Indian capital market is highly volatile, therefore there is an imperative need for the corporate clients to protect their operating profits by shifting the uncontrollable financial risks. In this content derivatives occupy an important place as a risk reducing machinery. Derivatives are useful to reduce the capital market risks. The derivatives ensure that risks can be hedged by using various derivative components, such as futures, options and swaps etc.

The derivatives derive their value from an underlying asset. The derivatives are based on all those financial instruments, which are explicitly traded in the stock exchanges such as equities, debt instruments, forex instruments and commodity based contracts.

A derivative is a financial product, which has been derived from market for another product. The derivatives have the objectives of hedging, speculation, price discovery, allocation of resources and transactional efficiency. There are three major players in the derivatives markets viz., hedgers, speculators and arbitrageurs. The derivative provides several advantages such as increased volumes, lower cost of transactions, hedging against risks and others. The derivatives also derive the risks such as credit risk market risk, legal risk, and operational risks.

10.9 Key words

Arbitrage

The simultaneous purchase and sale of similar commodities or securities such as derivatives in the hope of gaining from the price differentials.

Derivatives

A financial product which has been derived from another financial product or commodity.

Hedgers

The parties, which manage the risks by shifting the transaction to another party.

Hedge

The establishment of our opposite positions in the futures or options market from that held in the physical market as a protection against the possibility of adverse prices fluctuations.

Futures

Futures are agreements between two counter parties that fix the terms of an exchange.

Option

Option is a contract, which gives the holder right to purchase or sell the underlying future contracts (or) security at a specified period of time.

Swaptions

The option on swaps known as swaptions.

Volatility

A measure of a degree to which price fluctuations have occurred in the past can be expected to occur in the future.

10.10 Questions

Short Questions

1. Explain the concept of derivatives.
2. What are the advantages of derivatives?

3. Who are the players in the derivative market?
4. What are the risks of derivatives?

Essay Questions

1. Define derivatives, explain the need for the derivatives, markets in India.
2. Discuss the objectives and risks of derivatives in India.
3. Explain the recent trends in derivatives markets in India.

10.11 Suggested Readings

1. D.C.Gardener, *Futures and Options*, Indian Institute of Bankers, Macmillan, New Delhi, 1999.
2. V.Brahmarah and P. Subba Rao, *Financial Futures and Options*, HPH, Bombay, 1998.
3. Sugan Thomas, *Derivatives Markets in India*, Tata McGraw Hill Company, New Delhi, 1998.
4. Prof. V.Gangadhr, Management of Financial Derivatives, *The Chartered Accountant*, January, 2002.

11
FUTURES

OBJECTIVES

Following are the objectives of the lesson on futures:

- To discuss the Concept of Features and their Advantages of Futures.
- To Distinguish between Futures and Forward Contracts.
- To explain the Futures Market.
- To analyse the Components of futures such as Commodity Futures, Financial Futures and Stock Index Futures.
- To Present the Concept of Hedging and Its Advantages.

11.1 Introduction

Futures are agreements between two counter parties that fix the terms of an exchange. Futures are highly standardised contracts between the buyers and sellers or writers. Futures are not securities. Futures contract provides for the delivery of contracted assets. Futures markets are also called as "Paper Markets". Futures are traded in auction markets organised by futures exchanges. They are transferable legal agreements and their terms are not changed during the life of the contract. They create an obligation to make or take delivery at some future date. The trading is a kin to badla trading and it includes an interest component. The futures trading require only margin deposit and not the full payment immediately.

11.2 Definition of Futures

Futures can be defined as "a commitment to buy or sell at a specified future settlement date and a designated amount of a commodity or a financial asset. It is a legally binding contract by two parties to make or take delivery of a commodity at a certain point of time in future".

"A future contract is an agreement between a seller and buyer that calls for the seller to deliver to the buyer a specified quantity, grade of an identified commodity at a fixed time in the future and at a price agreed to when the contract is first entered into".

A future price incorporates the market belief about the likely course of assets underlying price. Futures contracts are transferable specific delivery forward contracts. Futures contracts are on stock indices and not on individual stocks. Futures contracts increase the liquidity. The futures contract period of time may be in between 3 to 21 months abroad. A future contract is a form of forward contract which conveys an agreement to buy or sell a specific amount of a commodity or financial instrument at a particular price on a stipulated future date. A future contract obligates the buyer to purchase the underlying instrument, and the seller to sell it, unless the contract is sold to another before settlement date, which may happen in order to take a profit or limit a loss.

Objectives of Future Contracts

Future contracts have the following Objectives:

(a) Hedging

(b) Speculation

(c) Price determination and discovery

(d) Efficient allocation of resources

The Salient Features of Futures Contract

The main features of futures contracts are presented below:

1. Futures are traded only in organised exchanges.
2. Futures contracts required having standard contract terms.
3. Futures exchanges have associated with clearing house.
4. Futures positions can be closed easily.
5. Regulatory authorities like SEBI regulate futures markets.

Various types of futures contracts are in practice in markets for commodities and financial instruments. The different types of contracts are as follows:

(A) Ready Delivery Contract

(B) Forward Delivery Contract

(A) Ready Delivery Contract

It provides for delivery of goods/instruments and payment of a price either immediately or within 11 days after the time of contract. It leads to spot or cash transactions, which take place at current prices of commodity.

(B) Forward Contract

It is a contract for delivery of the goods. These transactions are spot delivery of transactions. It is also known as "Specific delivery contract". They are deferred for execution to a future but fixed date.

11.3 Futures Vs. Forward Contracts

Futures and forward contracts are similar in many aspects.

But there are many differences between these contracts. Futures contracts have several transactional advantages relative to spot and forward contracts.

Futures Contract	*Forward Contract*
1) Trading is regulated.	1) Trading is not regulated.
2) Banks, Corporations, Individual Investors, Financial Institutions and Speculators are active participants.	2) Participants are institutions
3) Small amounts of money change hands.	3) No money changes hands until deliver.
4) Trading is in competitive environment like "bids, offers, auctions."	4) Trading will be done through telephone or telex
5) Settlements are made daily.	5) Settlement will be made at an agreed fixed dates in the future.
6) The delivery price is the spot price.	6) The delivery price is the forward price.
7) The contracts are standardised instruments.	7) The contracts are customerised.
8) These contracts have very small turnover.	8) These contracts are much larger turn over.
9) These contracts are traded in recognised exchanges.	9) These contracts can be traded on OTC and off-exchange.
10) There are secondary market services available.	10) There are no secondary market services available.

11.4 Futures Market

A futures contract is a standardised one. It is a standardised forward contract, it is legally enforceable and it is always traded on an organised exchange. According to Clark, futures trading can be defined as "A special type of future contract bought and sold under the rules of the organised exchanges". The term 'future trading' includes speculative transactions, where futures are bought and sold with a view to avoiding unforeseen losses resulting from price fluctuations.

Futures markets are among the most efficient and provide sound liquidity to the players. The buyers will compete with one another due involvement of large numbers and sellers also plenty. These are highly liquid markets and the spread between the buyer's bid prices and seller's asking prices at any time is driven by the competition. The size of the market, the liquidity and spread of the prices Is the good measures of the futures markets.

In the futures market standardised contractual agreements are bought and sold, but not the actual commodities. The futures contract is specific towards the quantity, quality and dates, but it does not involve immediate transfer of ownership of the commodity, unless it is treated in the spot delivery. One can buy and sell commodities in futures market regardless of whether or not he owns particular commodity.

Structure of the Futures Market

The settlement of all futures contracts is to be done in a futures market through an independent clearinghouse. The clearinghouse guarantees the performance of every contract traded in the exchange. For this purpose the clearinghouse insists on the margin system. The margins are collected in two different forms. An initial margin that will be deposited with the clearing house when a position is opened, and a daily system of payment based on movements of the daily futures prices. The system of margins permits the clearinghouse to guarantee the performance of all contracts. Therefore, the futures markets participants are need not to be worried with the counter party's credit worthiness. The result of this system is to provide a rare combination of a very high level of leverage with a low level of default risk. The successful futures markets usually have high underlying price volatility and a number of participants whose wealth is significantly exposed to the underlying price.

Characteristics of Futures

The main characteristics of futures are presented below:

1. There is limited number of actively traded products with futures contracts.
2. The trading unit is large and indivisible.
3. It has no more than maturity of 3 months.
4. The success ratio of new contracts is about 25% in the world financial markets.
5. Farmers seldom use futures.
6. There are both commercial and non-commercial users of futures contract in interest rates and foreign exchange transaction.
7. The main use of the futures by the commercials is to hedge corresponding cash and forward positions.
8. The position of the non-commercials is almost entirely speculative in nature.
9. In foreign exchange futures, the positions of the commercials are unbalanced.

11.5 Kinds of Futures

The following are the different kinds of futures:

(a) Commodity Futures

(b) Financial Futures

(c) Stock Index Futures

11.5(a) Commodity Futures

The commodity futures deal with trading in all domestic commodities. The value of commodity futures generally depends upon the price movements of market.

A commodity futures is a futures contract in commodities like agricultural products, metals, minerals etc. In an organised commodity futures markets, the contracts are standardised with standard quantities. They also have fixed delivery dates. In India commodity futures in agricultural products are popular.

A commodity is any product, service, financial instrument, or foreign currency that is bought and sold in recognised futures markets. The commodity futures are the predetermined contracts whose terms are defined by the exchange. There are about 100 commodities traded on different exchanges in USA and Europe. The following table presents the organised commodities exchanges.

Name of the Exchange		Commodities Traded
1. Chicago Board of Trade (CBT)	:	Various agricultural, metals and oils
2. Chicago Mercantile Exchange (CME)	:	Live Stock
3. International Monetary Exchange (IMF)	:	oreign currencies
4. London Metal Exchange (LMF)	:	Gold and other metals
5. Commodity Exchange New York (COMEX)	:	All varieties of agricultural commodities
6. International Petroleum Exchange of London (IPE)	:	Crude oil

11.5(b) Financial Futures

Futures contracts based on a financial investment or a financial index are known as financial futures.

Financial futures refer to a futures contract in foreign exchange or in financial instruments like treasury bills, commercial paper, stock market index or interest rate. In this futures markets the financial services.companies can play a very dynamic role. Financial futures are very popular in western countries as hedging instruments to protect against exchange rate/interest rate fluctuations and for ensuring future interest rates on loans.

Some of the well established financial futures exchanges are given below:

1. International Monetary Market (IMM) : Deals with US treasury bills, Eurodollar deposits, Sterling etc.
2. London International Financial Futures Exchange (LIFFE): Deals in Eurodollar deposits.
3. New York Futures Exchange (NYFE): Deals in sterling, Eurodollar deposits etc.

Financial futures can be classified into the following types:

1. Interest rate futures
2. Currency futures

1. Interest Rate Futures

These are written on the basis of interest rates or price indices of fixed interest securities.

2. Currency Futures

These futures are also called as "Foreign Exchange Futures". They are traded on the basis of prices of forex market. It deals with the price fluctuations of currency.

11.5(c) Stock Index Futures

Stock Index Futures contract is a contract based on stock indices. Stock index future is a speculation tool. Stock Index Futures were first introduced by Kansas City Board of Trade in 1982 in USA. Now these are most actively traded futures.

Stock Index Futures Contract is a futures contract on major stock market indices. This sort of contracts is very popular for speculators, investors and portfolio managers. They can hedge against future decline or increase in prices of portfolios depending upon the situation. The Stock Index Futures are successful, as they have proven to be useful to managing large stock portfolios. The increase in institutional investors including foreign institutional investors and their active trading are also responsible for the development of stock index futures trading.

It is an inexpensive and highly liquid asset in the market. It is a tool for expression of an opinion about the general situation of the market. These contracts are more useful to portfolio managers to alter the Risk-Return distribution of their portfolios. The institutional investors can enter the market immediately, by purchasing stock index contracts. A stock index futures contract is an obligation to deliver on the settlement date an amount of the agreed cash. No physical delivery of stocks is made to buyers. In order to ensure that sufficient funds are available for settlement, both buyers and sellers are required to put up a good faith deposit or margin. The margin is not a down payment, and neither loan nor margin interest are involved. The contract is marked to the market, daily and additional cash margin may be required depending upon the market movements. It is easy to see that the higher leverage afforded in the stock index futures market is an essential attraction to both buyers and sellers. For ex: "Assume a contract is struck at 600 and the index moves up as high as 675 and down as low 560 prior to expiration. During this time, funds are being debited and credited each day from buyer to seller". In stock index futures contract, everyday at the end of each trading session, each customer's position is marked to the latest settlement prices. Each customer's account is credited/debited according to price changes. If any variation is found, the customer has to adjust the cash. Sometimes the customers account shows any excess amount, that amount may be withdrawn by the customer. For ex: we are dealing with a "sensex" of 1800 contract. The original margin is Rs.20,000 and the maintenance margin is Rs.10,000. Assume the contract is struck up with sensex at 1800. The next day the sensex moves up to 1810. The buyer receives Rs.18000 from the seller" margin account [(1810-1800) x 1800]. If the sensex moves from 1800 to 1780, the buyer owes the seller Rs.36000 [1800 – 1780] x 1800.

Features of Stock Index Futures

The following are some of the features of Stock Index futures:

(i) Specifying certain set or number of stocks.

(ii) Selection of a base period

(iii) A rule is selected for combining the prices of the stocks included in the index to determine the value of the index in periods subsequent to the base period.

Valuation of Stock Index Futures

The valuation of stock index futures is very simple and easy. It is explained with simple example: *An investor wants to hold the BSE sensex scrip-30 for the next year. Then he will collect dividends, and his principal value will increase up or down with the index.* At some price for the futures index, the investor can get exactly the same return by investing in treasury bills and make purchase a contract for future delivery of the index.

$$\text{Return on Index} = \begin{matrix}\text{Index price}\\ \text{at expiration}\end{matrix} - \left(\text{Current index price} + \text{Dividends}\right)$$

$$= I_E - [I_B + D]$$

I_E = Index price at expiration

I_B = Current index price

D = Dividends

$$\text{Return on futures} = \begin{matrix}\text{Index price}\\ \text{at expiration}\end{matrix} - \left(\text{Current futures price} + \text{Dividends}\right)$$

$$= F_E - [F_B + R_F]$$

F_E = Futures price at expiration

F_B = Current future price

R_F = Interest on risk free rate of return

Therefore, the following formula expresses the value of stock index future.

$F_B = I_B + (R_f - D)$

F_B = Current future price

I_B = Current index price

R_f = Interest or Risk free rate of return

D = Dividend

The price of index should be equal to the price of futures at expiration.

Stock Index Arbitrage

Arbitrage means buying and selling of a commodity in two different markets in order to get profit from price fluctuations of the two markets. For ex: *If the price of the gold in Mumbai is Rs.5500 per 10 grams and the same in Chennai is Rs.5600, therefore, an opportunity exists to buy gold in Mumbai and sell in Chennai to earn a profit of Rs.100 per 10 grams.* Arbitrage makes market more efficient. Stock index arbitrage means buying a basket of stocks and selling futures contract. Arbitrage will play the most important role in the pricing of these contracts. In the pricing of futures, the index dividend and return on alternative investment should be kept in mind. Market sentiment also plays an important role in future pricing. However, every stock index arbitrage has its factors at that time such as amount of capital available, transaction costs, the rate of return available from the arbitrage.

11.6 Hedging

The main feature of a futures contract is to hedge against price fluctuations. The buyers of a futures contract hope to protect themselves from future spot price increases and the sellers from future spot price decreases.

Hedging is an activity of trading futures with the objective of reducing or controlling risk. Hedging is the counterbalancing of market commitments or positions to avoid or lessen the financial loss. The futures will provide natural hedging opportunity by establishing the relationship between the futures markets and cash markets. The hedging involves taking a position in futures that is opposite either to a position that is already had in the cash market or to a future cash obligation due to the entering into the forward contract.

The basic objective of the hedging is to minimise risk. However the hedger will enter into high risk with a view to earn higher profits.

Advantages of Hedging

The hedging in the futures market provides the business with a number of important advantages. The hedging substantially reduces the price risk in dealing with commodities or financial instruments, without effecting the normal business operations. It provides greater flexibility in planning, and permits easier and greater financing flexibility. The following are some of the main advantages of hedging.

(i) Hedging reduces the substantial price risks which are inherent in dealing with commodities and financial instruments.

(ii) Hedging does not affect the normal business operations. It provides for the substantial price protection.

(iii) It permits greater flexibility in planning futures market operations.

(iv) Hedging provides easier and greater financing facility.

Recent developments in futures trading

The commencement of futures trading in 31 individual scrips heightened sentiment on stock markets. NSE and BSE commenced futures trading on individual shares from 9.11.2001. On NSE, the total number of futures contact on individual securities traded was 4503 with a value of Rs.89.15 crores. L&T was the most active script with 1612 contracts being traded with a value of Rs.33.33 crores. Satyam Computers was the next most active futures contract with 593 contracts being traded with a value of Rs.10.69 crores. However, among the 31 scrips in many cases, futures were traded at discount to the cash market, even with the bullish mood in market.

The introduction of this product will place India among the few countries that allow trading on single stock futures. It is expected that the introduction of leveraged product like single stock futures will inject the much needed liquidity into the Indian capital market as different products allow traders to carry forward their positions while taking a more long term view of the market.

Moreover, stock futures will throw open up hedging and arbitrage opportunities to all market participants. Since, there are number of products based on the same underlying shares, there will be arbitrage opportunities between the underlying cash market, single stock futures and stock option.

11.7 Summary of the Lesson

Futures are the one of the components of the financial derivatives. The futures are highly standardised contracts between buyers and sellers or writers. Futures are not the securities but which are derived based on the underlying financial assets. The futures price incorporates belief into the market about the likely course of assets underlying price. Futures contracts are transferable specific delivery forward contracts. The futures contracts will have the objectives such as hedging, speculation, price determination and discovery and efficient allocation of resources. There is wide variety of differences between futures contract and forward contracts.

Futures markets are most efficient and provide sound liquidity to the players. The futures are divided into commodity futures, financial futures and stock index futures. Hedging is an activity of trading futures with the objective of reducing or controlling risks. There are several advantages of the hedging such as substantial reduction of price risks, does not affect the normal business operations, and provides greater flexibility in planning the operations and greater financing facility.

11.8 Key words

1. Basis	:	The difference between cash and futures prices for the same commodity.
2. Clearing house	:	The organisation, which assures the financial integrity of futures and options market by guaranteeing obligations money among its clearing numbers.
3. Expiration date	:	The date on which an option or future contract expires.
4. Forward contract	:	In which two parties agree to buy or sell an asset in some future date under the conditions, which are mutually agreeable.
5. Futures Contract	:	An agreement to make or take delivery of a standardised amount of a commodity during a specific month, at a price established by open auction on a trading floor.
6. Hedging	:	The process of off-setting the price risks inherent in any cash market position by taking an opposite position in the futures or option market.
7. Margin	:	The amount of money a customer has to deposit when establishing a futures or option

		position to guarantee their contract obligations.
8. Off-set	:	The liquidation of a futures or option contract through the purchase or sale of an identical contract.
9. Spread	:	The price difference between two futures or options contracts.
10. Volatility	:	A measure of the amount by which an asset's price fluctuated over a given period

11.9 Questions

1. Distinguish between futures contract and forward contract.
2. What are the features and advantages of futures contract?
3. What are the futures? Discuss the position of futures markets in India?
4. What are the different types of futures? Explain them with suitable examples?
5. What is hedging? What are its advantages?
6. What do you understand by stock index futures? Explain how do you value the stock index futures?

11.10 Books for further Reading

1. Susan Thomas, *Derivatives Markets in India*, Tata McGraw Hill, New Delhi, 1998.
2. Brahmaiah & Subba Rao, *Financial Futures and Options*, HPH Bombay, 1998.
3. Prof. V. Gangadhar, Management of Financial Derivatives, *The Journal of Chartered Accountant*, January-2002.

12
OPTIONS AND SWAPS

OBJECTIVES

The objectives of this lesson are to

- explain the concepts, types and features of options and swaps.
- discuss methods for valuation of options
- present the definition, features and usefulness of warrants
- analysing the nature of convertible securities
- discuss the features and usefulness of convertible debentures.

12.1 Introduction

An option is a contract, which involves the right to buy or sell securities at specified prices within a stated time. Option is a device for the gains from speculation, "An option is a type of contract between two parties". Option is a component of derivative securities used for the purpose of risk management in the investment. The longest option period is 9 months, but it can be for a shorter period of 30 to 90 days. The contract unit can be of 100 shares or stocks. The minimum trading unit can be fixed at 100 contracts. The options are credited and traded by the investors. The companies, which issue assets underlying them, have no responsibility in respect of their creation.

12.2 Definition of Options

According to D.C. Gardener "An option is a contract which conveys to the owner the right, but not the obligation to buy or sell a particular stock at a specified price on a given data. The seller of the option gives the right. "

Susan Thomas in her book on Derivatives Markets in India states that "An option is a legal contract that gives the holder the right to buy or sell a specified amount of the underlying, interest at a fixed or determinable price upon exercise of the option.

Amitab Baxi defines "An option is a contract conveying the right but not obligation to buy or sell a specified financial instruments at a fixed price before or at a certain future data".

Thus, based on the above definitions it can be pointed out that an option contract imposes obligation on only one party. The contract gives the buyer the right but not the obligation to purchase or sell, a stated quantity of underlying commodity at some point of time in the future at a price agreed.

12.3 Characteristics of Options

The following are the characteristics of options:

(i) Option holders do not receive any interest or dividend

(ii) Options yield only capital gains

(iii) Options holder can enjoy a tax advantage

(iv) Options are traded on O.T.C. and in all recognised stock exchanges.

(v) Options holders can control their rights on underlying asset.

(vi) Options create the possibility of gaining a windfall profit.

(vii) Options can enjoy a much wider risk-return combinations

(viii) Options can reduce the total portfolio transaction costs

(ix) Options enable with the investors to gain better returns with a limited amount of investment.

In options trading, exercise date means, the date on which the buyer actually exercises the option. It is the price at which the option holder can buy or sell the underlying asset. Exercise price is also called as "striking price". The options are mainly classified into following two types:

(a) Call option

(b) Put option

(a) Call Option

A call option gives the right to buy shares under a negotiable contract and which does not carry any obligation. The buyers have the right to receive the delivery of asset is known as "call option".

(b) Put Option

In this option the owner is the right to sell the underlying asset under a negotiable contract Put-option holder has the right to receive the payment by surrendering the asset.

The writer of an option is a stockbroker or a security dealer. The buyer of an option pays a price depending on the risk of the underlying security.

12.4 Kinds of Options

There are a wide variety of options available in the market. They are:

(a) Commodity option

(b) Currency option

(c) Stock option

(d) Stock index option

(a) Commodity Option

Commodity option enables the formers to trade in general commodities market movements. They are traded based upon consumption goods. The price movement of commodities will respect the worth of commodity option.

(b) Currency Option

The recent addition to options markets is the foreign currency exchange or currency options. It acts as a vehicle to project against adverse exchange rate fluctuations. These are the contracts, which confer the right to buy or sell foreign currency at a specified price at some future date. The latest innovation in this context is the futures option a combination of futures and options.

(c) Stock Option

A complex variety options exists in the market Stock option is one of the options. Stock option may be on an individual stock or an various stock price indices. The stock option requires the actual delivery of stock up on exercise. The stock option is costly to some extent, while comparing with stock index option. It involves mostly individual stock or group of stocks.

(d) Stock Index Option

Stock index option enables investors to trade on general stock market movements. The stock prices movement will reflects in stock index option prices. In stock index option the transactions are settled by payments of cash. The amount of cash settlement is equal to the difference between the closing price of the index option price and the strike price of the option. The investment strategies with index options are similar to those for individual stock options.

Features of Options

The following are the main features of options:

(i) The option is exercisable only by the owner namely the buyer of the option.

(ii) The owner has limited liability.

(iii) Owners of options have no voting rights and dividend right.

(iv) Options have high degree of risk to the option writers.

(v) Options involving buying counter position by the option sellers.

(vi) Flexibility in investors needs.

(vii) The company issues no certificates.

(viii) Options are popular because they allow the buyer profits from favourable moments in exchange rate.

A wide variety of terms are used in options trading in the market. These are presented below:

(a) call option

(b) put option

(c) writing option

(d) spread option

(e) gale options

(f) double options

a) Call Option

A call option provides the buyer right to buy shares under a negotiable contract and which do not carry any obligation.

b) Put Option

In the put option the owner is the right to sell the underlay asset under a negotiable contracts.

c) Writing Option

Writing of an option can be in two kinds:

(i) Covered option

(ii) Uncovered option

Covered option is written against an owned stock position, uncovered option may be written without owning the securities.

d) Spread Option

The price differences between two option contracts are called spread option. It is the process, which involves the simultaneous purchase and sale of different options of the same security. Spread options may be two kinds:

(a) Vertical spread

(b) Horizontal spread

Vertical spread involves purchase of two options with the same expiry date but different striking prices. In the horizontal spread, the striking price is the same but expiry dates are different.

Options may be purchased or sold by placing an order with a broker. An innovative development in options is eliminating a physical instrument in option trading. In options dealing no certificate is issued. This facilitates prompt settlement of transactions. In the absence of a certificate, each transaction and associated money activities must be handled as a bookkeeping entry.

Option prices are the result of the interaction of a number of different forces. There are six fundamental factors, which influence the value of an option.

(a) Current stock price (s)

(b) Striking price (k)

(c) Time to expiration (t)

(d) Stock volatility (stock prices fluctuation)

(e) Rates of interest

(f) Cash dividends

The striking price depends upon current stock price and the expiration date. The higher the stock price, the higher the call values. The stock volatility is an important determinant in value of an option. The higher volatility in stock market, then the stock will do either very well or very poor. Therefore, the higher volatile over the lifetime of a call, the higher will be its value relative to the stock. The another important determinant of a factor is "interest rates". The Higher interest rate, the lower the values of the striking price. Higher interest rate will have the same influence as a lower striking price. Higher interest rates tend to imply higher call prices. Cash dividends are also play an important factor in valuation of an option. The higher the cash dividends prior to expiration, the higher the value of a put option.

Option strategies may be for hedging, speculation or spreading purposes. Hedging in option involves attempts to control risk. Speculation in options requires the purchase or the sale of an option without any position in the underlying stock. Spreading requires that the simultaneous purchase of one option and the sale of another. The person doing the spreading is hedging Spreading may be categorised as:

(a) Bullish spread

(b) Bearish spread

Bullish spread involves in buying the more expansive option and selling the cheaper option. The spread will show a profit if the price rise. In bearish spread, a profit is anticipated if the stock price declines. Using makes valuation of an option. "The Black-Scholes Model" . Black and Scholes have developed a device, which assumes that the share returns are normally distributed. Let us examine how the Black-Schole Model is useful in valuation of an option.

Black-Scholes Model

Black and Scholes developed a formula for determining the value of an option. The model is very popular in the market and is useful to option holder to know the over priced or under priced of an asset. The model provides an excellent analysis in valuation of debt relation to equity. The equilibrium value of an option can be determined by the following assumptions:

1. There is no dividend payment on shares
2. There is no interruption in market operations
3. There are no transaction costs
4. There are no taxes
5. The share prices are not in volatile position
6. The interest rates are constant
7. The option is to be European type

The Black-Scholes formula for estimating the fair value of call option.

$$V_c = P_s\,[Nd_1] - P_x/(e^{(RF)(T)})\ [Nd_2]$$

$$d_1 = \frac{I_n(\frac{P_s}{P_x}) + T\,(RF - \frac{\sigma^2}{2})}{\sigma\sqrt{T}} \qquad d_2 = \frac{I_n(\frac{P_s}{P_x}) + T\,(RF - \frac{\sigma^2}{2})}{\sigma\, T}$$

$$d_2 = d_1 - \sigma\sqrt{T}$$

P_s = The exercise price of the call option.

e = 2.7183 – base to the natural logarithm

RF = Compounded annual risk free rate

σ = The standard deviation of the continuously compounded annual rate of return on the shares.

P_x = The current price of the share

I_n = The natural log of the bracket number

T = The time remaining to expiration on annual basis

Nd_1 & Nd_2 = The value of the cumulative normal distribution at d_1 and d_2

d_1 & d_2 = The dividends received in year 1 and 2

After taking the dividends into consideration, the formula (Block Schole) should be as follows:

$$P_s = P_s - \sum_{e=1}^{T} Dt/e^{RFxt}$$

P_s = The current price of the share

P_s = Adjusted stock price

D_1 = Declared/known cash dividend to be paid on day t from now.

The Valuation of an Option based on European Model

The valuation of an option on the basis of European model can be as presented by incorporating the Block and Scholes call price

$$P_p = \frac{P_x}{e^{rft}} N(-d_2) - P_s N(-d_1)$$

(OR)

$$P_p = -P_s N{-}d_1 + \frac{P_x}{e^{rft}} N - d_2$$

P_p = Put call parity

12.5 Definition of Swaps

A swap is yet another exciting trading instrument. It is one of the component of financial derivatives. Swap is a combination of forwards by two counter points. It is arranged to reap the benefits arising from the fluctuations in the market. According to A.K. Seth, "A swap is an agreement between two or more people/parties to exchange sets of cash flows over a period in future".

Swaps are agreements between two parties to exchange assets at pre-determined intervals.

According to D.C. Gardner a swap can be defined as "the exchange of one stream of future cash flows with another stream of cash flows with different characteristics", Swaps are generally customerised transactions. The swaps are innovative financing instruments, which reduce borrowing costs, and increase control over interest rate risk and forex explosive. Swaps are useful in avoiding the problem of unfavourable fluctuations in forex market. The corporates, commercial banks, institutional investors, individual investors are now using the swaps more frequently. The swaps include both spot and forward transactions in a single agreement. The following factors have been influenced for the growth of swap market in India.

(a) Deregulation of financial policies

(b) Growing global financial integration

(c) Increasing volatility of interest and exchange rates

The swaps are associated with equity indices and physical commodities, like oil and oil products. Swaps are concerned with exchange rates or interest rates. Swaps can penetrate savings in perfectly at free market. Financial swaps are revolutionary especially for portfolio management. A swap, which is coupled with an existing asset or liability can radically, modifies effective risk and return. Swaps have had a major macro economic impact foregoing the linkage between the Euro and domestic markets.

12.6 Types of Swaps

The swaps can be divided into following types:

(a) Currency swaps

(b) Interest rate Swaps

(a) The currency swaps

These are the agreements whereby currencies are exchanged at specified intervals. The currency swaps would involve creation of a fund in one currency for a predetermined time for whatever purpose by exchanging the source fund into the derived fund. Therefore, exchange contract is entered into, to convert the derived fund back into source fund, which covers the principal amounts together with their respective interest at maturity. These are arranged for periods ranging from two to ten years with a maturity of five years. Thus, the currency swaps entail the borrowing of one currency and lending of another as well as the spot purchase of one currency with another and forward sale of the currency for the other.

(b) Interest Rate swaps

An interest rate swap is an agreement whereby one party exchanges one set of interest rate payment for another rate over a time period. The swaps, which transform interest flows from fixed to floating in the same currency, are called interest rate swaps. The interest rates are calculated an national values of principals.

12.7 Warrants

A stock purchase warrant or a warrant is a call option issued by the firm whose stock serves as a underlying securities. A warrant usually has a longer time to expiration beyond a period of 5 years than a typical call option. A warrant is a component of financial derivative. Warrant is a corporate created option to purchase a stated number of common shares at a specified price within a specified time. Warrants are attached to bonds/ debentures and equity issues. Warrants generally have long term maturity. Warrants help companies in raising fresh capital. Warrants can be detached and traded separately. The maturity period of warrants is 3 to 10 years. Perpetual warrants are available abroad. Warrants are similar to call options with little differences. Companies issue warrants and options are created by investors. Warrants are issued for long-period basis but options expire within nine months. Options are standardised but warrants are not.

A warrant holder has no equity rights in the firm. He does not receive dividends and does not have voting rights. Warrants are issued in the ratio determined by the company such as one warrant per one share. The difference between the actual price of a warrant and its minimum value is called as "premium". The warrant value depends upon the stock potential for rising the prices. High dividend pay out may also have an adverse effect on the price of a warrant. Many investors purchase the warrants for speculative purpose only. Warrant market is a gamblers market. Warrants provide benefit to the following:

A) Corporate sector

B) Investors

A) Corporate sector

The following are the benefits to the corporate sector;

1. Warrants facilitate to raise funds to the corporate sector.

2. There is no obligation to pay interest and repayment of principal.

3. Issues of warrants do not have floatation costs

B) Advantages to the Investors

The following are the advantages to the investors.

(a) Low amount of investment

(b) Provide greater liquidity due to marketability

(c) Facilitates for capital grains.

The following formula can be used to value the a warrants

$$P_w = f[P_o, T_m, P_c, D_i, F_c]$$

P_w = Market price of the warrant

P_o = Option price of the equity price

P_c = Current price of the equity share

T_m = Duration of the issue

D_i = The ratio between shares outstanding and warrants

F_c = The equity share price

The warrants can also be valued with the help of the following formula:

$$V = [P_c - P_o] N$$

V = The value of a warrant

P_c = Current price of the equity share

P_o = Option price of the equity share

N = No. of shares may be purchased with one warrant

12.8 Convertible Securities

The convertible securities are very popular financial instruments, which can be converted into different security of the same firm under certain conditions. The typical case involves bond or debentures preference shares, convertible into equity shares of a company with a stated number of shares received for each bond or a preference share. In the case of convertible securities no cash is involved. The old securities are traded in the stock exchange and appropriate number of new securities is issued in return.

The convertible securities often contain a call provision, which may be used by the corporation to force conversion when stock market price is sufficiently high to make the value of the stock obtained on conversion exceed the call price of the bond.

In the convertible securities, convertible bonds or convertible debentures are more popular because these are a hybrid securities. The debentures may be converted into equity shares after a fixed period. Until this period the convertibles carry interest as usual. The investments are more attractive as compared to fixed deposits. Convertible debentures combine high rate of return with the profitability of capital appreciation and the liquidity of shares. The main features of convertible debentures are presented below:

1. Conversion prices
2. Conversion ratio
3. Amount of conversion
4. Convertible value
5. Investment value of a debenture
6. Timing of conversion
7. Premium
8. Market price

1. *Conversion Price*

The debentures are converted into equity shares at the end of a specific period. The ratio at which the convertible debentures are exchanged for equity shares is known as conversion price. For ex: if the face value of a convertible debenture is Rs.100/- and it is convertible into 2 equity shares of Rs.50/- each, the conversion price is Rs.50/- and the conversion ratio is 2. The face value of equity is Rs.10/- and the remaining Rs.40/- is the premium.

2. *Conversion Ratio*

The conversion ration indicates the number of equity shares is to be issued for each convertible bond. For ex. If a company goes for a public issue of 15% convertible bonds of Rs.350 each for cash at par. Each bond face value is Rs.350 and had a conversion price of Rs.175. The conversion ratio is 2. i.e. Rs.350 ÷ 175 = 2.

		price, on or before a fixed date, a fixed quantity.
3. Strike or exercise price	:	Fixed price at which the option may be exercised and the underlying asset bought or sold.
4. American option	:	The buyer can only exercise the option at any time before the date of maturity.
5. European option	:	The option can only be exercised by the buyer on the maturity date and not before the maturity date.
6. Forward contract	:	A deferred contract in which two parties agree to buy and sell an asset at some future time under conditions that are mutually agreeable.
7. Option writer	:	The person who sells or grants an option in return for a premium and who is obligated to perform if the option holder exercise his right under the option contract.
8. Speculator	:	The trader whose objective is to make profits by successfully anticipating future price.

12.12 Questions

Short Questions

1. Define an option.
2. What are call and put options?

A credit linked note : It is another type of credit derivatives. It is a combination of a regular bond and a credit option. This note assures to make regular interest payments. It also promises to pay a large amount, when the bond matters. The credit derivatives can reduce credit risk but also they expose the users of new financial risks. Credit derivatives are privately negotiable financial contracts.

12.10 Summary

There are different types of derivatives. The popular among them are futures, options, swaps, warrants and convertible securities. An option is a legal contract that gives the holder right to buy or sell a specified amount of the underlying interest at a fixed or determinable price upon exercise of option. The options can be classified into call option and put option. The call option gives the right to buy the securities as per the contract and which does not carry any obligation, whereas in put option the owner is the right to sell the underlying asset entered in the contract. There are different types of options such as commodity option, currency option, stock option and stock index option. A swap is at another exciting trading instrument. Swap is a combination of forwards by two counter parties. A swap can be defined as the exchange of one stream of future cash flows with another stream of cash flows with different characteristics. Further, the swaps can be divided into currency swaps and interest rate swaps. A warrant is a call option issued by the firm whose stock serves as an underlying security. The convertible securities are very popular financial instruments, which can be converted into equity shares. The popular convertible securities are convertible bonds, debentures and preference shares.

12.11 Key Words

1. Call option : The right to buy at a fixed price, on or before a fixed date, a fixed quantity
2. Put option : The right to sell at a fixed